text by Nancy D'Oench
coordination by Bonny Martin
photography by Mick Hales

Abrams, New York
in association with
The Garden Club of America

GARDENS
private & personal

A Garden Club of America Book

Contents

Preface

THE GARDEN CLUB OF AMERICA HAS A LONG AND DISTINGUISHED HISTORY IN THE documentation of notable gardens. Shortly after the organization's founding in 1913, a Historic Gardens Committee was named to document and preserve photographic records of outstanding gardens. Between 1920 and 1935, more than 2,000 glass lantern slides of gardens were commissioned. Many were then hand-colored by the artist Edward van Altena. This project made the Garden Club of America one of the prime sponsors of early garden photography, offering little-known woman photographers such as Mattie Edwards Hewitt and Jessie Tarbox Beal an opportunity to pursue a genteel and respected artistic career.

The slides were used for Garden Club of America programs and, in 1927, a slideshow of American gardens at the English Speaking Union in London resulted in a request for more the next year.

In the 1930s, the interest in preserving a historic record of gardens inspired Alice G. B. Lockwood, a founding member of the organization, to write a two-volume illustrated history, *Gardens of Colony and State: Gardens and Gardeners of the American Colonies and of the Republic before 1840.* The *American Magazine of Art* hailed the publication of the first volume: "The historical facts set forth in this volume give glimpses of what has been, of the zeal and the ardor, the love of nature and beauty, with which our forebears planted and tended their gardens." The Garden Club of America reprinted the two-volume set in 2000 to mark the millennium.

In the 1980s, some of the glass slides commissioned in the early part of the century were rediscovered in the GCA archives. A committee researched and identified as many as possible, recovered many that had been dispersed, and began adding 35mm images of significant contemporary gardens. In 1987, 3,000 glass lantern slides and more than 22,000 35mm slides were presented to the Smithsonian Institution's Archives of American Gardens. Many of the glass slides were used to illustrate the entertaining and extensively researched book *The Golden Age of American Gardens: Proud Owners, Private Estates, 1890-1940* by Mac Griswold and Eleanor Weller (Harry N. Abrams, 1991).

These glass and 35mm slides—now known as the Garden Club of America Collection at the Archives of American Gardens, Smithsonian Institution—document more than 5,500 gardens and landscapes, including a large number of gardens in this book. Access to the archives is through the website www.siris.si.edu.

Gardens are a visual art form, and today's photography and reproduction have taken their documentation to new heights. It is in the spirit of preserving a visual record of outstanding American gardens and making it available to the reading public that we approached *Gardens Private and Personal,* asking members to open the gates of their private gardens.

Which gates? Which gardens? The Garden Club of America is currently composed of 197 clubs, whose members number more than 17,000. It is not an exaggeration to say that virtually every one of those 17,000 members has a garden that contains some vista, plant, or feature worthy of photographing. How, then, were the ninety-plus gardens featured in this book chosen? One would expect Bonny Martin, who coordinated the photographing of the gardens, to say, "With great difficulty." Instead, she says that it was not as hard as one would think. Margaret L. Kaplan, our editor at Abrams, first broached the idea of a book on members' gardens when Bonny, Mick Hales, and I were working on *The Fine Art of Flower Arranging* (2002). In the intervening years, the selection was never far from Bonny's mind. She knew many of the outstanding gardens across the country firsthand from decades of attending meetings and going on garden tours, and she queried authorities and members with similar experience in many parts of the country. Club and area representatives of two GCA committees proved especially helpful—the Visiting Gardens Committee and the Garden History and Design Committee. While all garden owners who were contacted were happy to have their garden photographed and included, a small number asked that we omit their names. We have respected their request.

The logistical challenge was to arrange for several outstanding gardens in one area to be available—and in their prime—at the same time so that Mick Hales could fly into a nearby airport and photograph. Bonny's phone calls numbered in the hundreds, and Mick's frequent flyer miles ran into the tens of thousands. My husband, Woody, and I met Mick at twenty of the gardens—in Atlanta, Houston, Dallas, and five different areas of California. My admiration for Mick's talent was joined by my awe at his stamina, focus, and perseverance. We are all grateful he survived our naïveté in understanding how much time and energy is required for air travel, car rentals, and being in one garden at sunrise and catching the last light of the day in perhaps a third or fourth garden. And we are especially grateful for the product—hundreds of beautiful photographs of exceptional gardens.

From that bounty, Margaret Kaplan and I selected 250 to illustrate the features a garden visitor might encounter—from entrance gates to flower borders to the occasional chicken coop. Then the garden owners were asked to tell their garden's story, to tell the readers what they might tell a visitor about its history, trials and tribulations, and pleasures. The written responses surprised and thrilled me. Given the opportunity to reflect on their gardens, the owners responded eloquently—with candor, warmth, humor, and, most especially, a deep love of their gardens. In many instances the pleasure in the garden was palpable; the words almost jumped off the page. It was abundantly clear that these able, knowledgeable people could have directed their talents and energy toward any number of pursuits, but had chosen to create and maintain a beautiful garden—and simply loved doing it. Excerpts from their essays appear near photographs of their gardens throughout the book.

Nancy D'Oench

Introduction

"Gardeners are friendly, generous people. Their willingness to share has taught me a very valuable lesson about being open to requests to visit our garden. Every request is an opportunity presenting itself—to learn and to add to a widening circle of gardening friends."

VIRGINIA ISRAELIT, PORTLAND, OREGON

"Gardeners are the most sharing people on earth. They can hardly wait to tell you about the newest and most exciting thing they've learned. No hoarding knowledge in this group."

JEANNE WILL, CHESTER, NEW JERSEY

YOU ARE ABOUT TO MEET MORE THAN NINETY GARDENERS WHO ARE HAPPY TO welcome visitors to their gardens. All of them have opened their garden gates to tours in the past and plan to do so in the future.

Gardening stands as one of the nation's most popular pastimes, passionately pursued by millions and accounting for billions of dollars in sales of plants, supplies, services, equipment, and, yes, books. But in addition to the millions of gardeners who relish the feel of damp soil in their hands and consider a tired back and creaking joints badges of honor for a good day of weeding and transplanting, there are many thousands more who appreciate the fruits of those labors. They may not pull weeds or spread compost, but they join the gardening millions in celebrating what each season presents in the garden: They are encouraged by the emergence of new shoots in the spring; they gladly stop, linger over, and smell the flowers of summer; they stand in awe as the green leaves of maples take on the flaming colors of autumn; and they can be stilled by the silhouette of bare branches against the winter sky. They are the garden lovers if not the garden doers.

The greatest of pleasures for these combined numbers is a garden tour, the opportunity to visit private gardens that are opened only on rare occasions for charity purposes. It is to these—the gardeners and the appreciative spectators of gardening—that we offer this book. It is a singular occasion to look over the garden wall, to pass through the gate, to enjoy the view, to wander the paths that lead from one garden room to the next—to glimpse into more than ninety private gardens lovingly tended by members of the Garden Club of America. As we visit, the owners will tell us how their gardens have evolved, show prize plants, recall disasters, point us toward a favorite resting spot. They may even give away secrets, such as how ice cubes helped hold the tulip blossoms until the day of the garden tour. And yes, they will wish we had come last week before the heavy rains and promise that if we could come back next week, the roses should be at their peak.

Looking at the images captured by master photographer Mick Hales, it is hard to believe any moment in these gardens could be better. We first met Mick when he recorded the ephemeral art of a hundred flower arrangers for the Garden Club of America book *The Fine Art of Flower Arranging*. Internationally recognized, his garden and architectural photography appears often in *House and Garden, House Beautiful,* and *Veranda.* The sole photographer for two dozen books, Mick has done both the commentary and the photography for *Monastic Gardens* (2000), *Gardens Around the World: 365 Days* (2004), *Shakespeare in the Garden* (2006), and *The Book of Psalms* (2008). He is the most knowledgeable of garden visitors and our guide on this tour of gardens from Maine to Hawaii, and from Palm Beach, Florida, to Seattle, Washington.

Visiting private gardens and taking a garden tour is not a modern phenomenon. Patrick Taylor in *The Oxford Companion to the Garden* (2006) tells us that Louis XIII of France admitted visitors to his Jardin Royal des Plantes Medicinales (now the Jardin des Plantes) in 1640 and even allowed a lemonade seller to cater to visitors' thirst. In England in the eighteenth century it was understood that, as a matter of noblesse oblige, any respectable person might be permitted to visit the grand estates, with the housekeeper answering their questions about the history of the house and garden. The Sixth Duke of Devonshire instructed his staff to turn on the fountains for visitors "irrespective of social class."

In Jane Austen's *Pride and Prejudice,* there is a scene in which Elizabeth Bennet and her aunt and uncle tour Mr. Darcy's estate. The housekeeper welcomes them warmly, gives a commentary on the artwork in the manor house—and on what a fine man Mr. Darcy is—and invites them to enjoy the grounds.

While most tourists to Europe and Asia now seek out historic gardens, visitors in the sixteenth and seventeenth centuries, according to *The Oxford Companion to the Garden,* were looking at relatively new gardens to see what design elements and unusual plant materials were employed. They brought home ideas and, often, actual plants; the Low Countries were known as a great source of trees for avenues. Visitors to France were eager to view the Baroque landscapes of André Le Nôtre. Visitors to Italy from France, Scotland, and Germany wrote detailed descriptions of Villa d'Este, Villa Farnese, Villa Lante, and other Renaissance gardens as they looked in the late 1500s, when the gardens were a mere decade or two old.

By the mid-eighteenth century, so many people were visiting Viscount Cobham's gardens at Stowe, England, that he had a guide published, probably to relieve the staff of answering questions (Thomas Jefferson stopped by in 1786). Comprehensive guides to notable estates in Italy were published at about the same time, reflecting the popularity of gardens with travelers making the Grand Tour.

Many of the aforementioned gardens are now the historic ones travelers seek out on their visits to Italy, France, or England. They are open to the public under the auspices of the National Trust in England—which oversees 200 historic homes and gardens—and similar agencies in other countries. But the opening of historic gardens to the public has not diminished the desire to see private gardens; in fact, it seems to have increased it, and Britain has made a unique response, capitalizing on this desire. In 1927, Miss Elsie Wagg of the Queen's Nursing Institute wanted to raise funds for her charity. She persuaded a few people to open their gardens for a small fee. From that beginning has grown the National Gardens Scheme. Its annual "Yellow Book," *Gardens of England and Wales Open for Charity,* lists more than 3,300 private gardens open to the public. Ticket revenues yield the equivalent of more than $3 million a year for charities. Every year, another 400 private gardens in Scotland open their gates under Scotland's Garden Scheme.

In the United States, thousands of organizations—from garden clubs and YMCAs to historical societies and botanical gardens—organize tours of private gardens as fund-raisers. These are widely advertised—the more visitors, the more money. One organization, the Garden Conservancy, has carried the visiting of private gardens to new and accessible heights in America. Founded in 1989 by Francis H. Cabot, it has, since 1995, held Open Days, America's only national garden visiting program. The annually published *Open Days Directory* includes descriptions, visiting dates, and locations of more than 300 outstanding private gardens coast to coast. Garden admissions are divided between the garden host's local charities and the work of the Conservancy, which is to support the preservation of exceptional gardens (www.GardenConservancy.org).

The first garden to benefit from the Garden Conservancy's support was the Ruth Bancroft Garden in Walnut Creek, California. There are now sixteen gardens under the Garden Conservancy's umbrella, some open to the public on a regular basis and all open on that area's Open Days. Many of the private gardens featured in this book have been on Open Days tours, some four and five times.

Today's visitors seek out gardens for the same reasons people sought them out in earlier centuries—for the pure enjoyment of the garden art and for learning, getting ideas, and seeing what plant materials are being used and how. Cabot, creator of five extraordinary gardens, assures us there's no cause for apology. In responding to a comment about his borrowing from other times and climes, he said, "But then, plagiarism is the lifeblood and the principal impetus in the creation of gardens. There is no more agreeable challenge than adapting someone else's good idea to one's own surroundings."

We believe you will find good ideas among these images and will find nuggets of wisdom in the garden owners' stories. Gardening, as defined by the participants in this book, is not a narrow subject. In addition to the fields of horticulture and garden design that come immediately to mind, gardening for many encompasses environmental responsibility—pesticide-free organic gardening, low-water xeriscaping, preserving and reintroducing native plant material, reducing energy consumption. Many see themselves as stewards of the historic gardens they now tend or of the land they are privileged to plan and plant. Some speak of preserving open space and deeding to land trusts. All hint at the related learning and appreciation of a range of subjects such as the interlocking ecology of the nearby bay, river, lake, or sound and the land reaching out from it; or the history of plant exploration and the art of botanical illustration. These were undercurrents in their stories. On the surface was simply the pure joy of being in the garden, expressed in so many ways, from Pat Hartrampf's "My love of gardening has led me down more primrose paths than I care

to acknowledge!" to Jeanne Will's reflection on her life in the garden: "I knew early on that horticulture in its many manifestations could infuse our lives with newness and beauty and surprises and challenges and solace and spiritual growth. It was part hard labor and part library research and part sheer bliss. Above all, the wonderful fellow gardeners I met along the way ratified this choice."

It is a choice reflected in the gardens featured here. You are invited to join the many visitors who have walked through these gardens and, although no previous experience is necessary, an observation from one who has seen thousands of visitors in gardens might be welcome. In his book *The Greater Perfection*, Francis H. Cabot says: "There is an art to visiting a garden and I have learned its characteristics by watching those who are good at it. One must take ample time to drink in each element and its relation to the garden as a whole as well as to the surrounding landscape. This approach not only takes considerable extra time, sitting reflectively where benches permit; it is best done alone, or in silence, with no more than one or two equally introspective companions. . . . The greatest of all compliments is when a visitor responds to the beauty encompassing the garden and its settings by shedding a tear. Now there is a soul mate!"

As you enter the gardens on these pages through Mick Hales's sensitive photography, we wish you a quiet, introspective journey and we hope you return often—to savor one page, one element at a time. The creators and maintainers of these treasures, each a paradise on earth, will say, "Now, there's a soul mate!"

above ✤ This gazebo in Sue McKinley's Montecito, California, garden is a bit removed from the house, making it an enticing destination for guests—who are rewarded with a superb view of the Mediterranean-style garden. Custom built of wrought iron and designed for entertaining up to forty guests, the structure has an electrified chandelier to enhance the candlelight.

1 An Invitation to Come In

GATES, DOORWAYS, AND GARDEN ENTRANCES ALL HINT AT WHAT LIES AHEAD AND give a promise of things to come. They can be as versatile as the rewards on the other side, the only caution being, according to Gertrude Jekyll in *Garden Ornament* (1918), that an "honest relation must exist between the entry and what is entered."

The gates to the Houston residence pictured here certainly meet that criterion. They let you know you are about to enter a grand and formal space. The recently constructed home just beyond the gates could be a *hôtel particulier*—a grand private house in early eighteenth-century Paris.

An open gate, such as the one to Langdon Farm on the Chesapeake Bay, is an invitation to another time and place. Just beyond the gate, an avenue of pines, beeches, and maples leads to a Georgian Revival house and to farm buildings dating from a 1659 Maryland land patent.

A gate can conceal as well as reveal. It may draw attention to itself while subtly screening what lies beyond. Such is the case with the gate designed and crafted by Ernest Weiman for Read's Leap, the Napa Valley property of Mary and Steven Read. With its gilt grape leaves, birds, and roses, it is a stunning garden ornament in its own right.

Once through the front gate, the doorway to the house repeats the message or, if there is no gate, speaks it clearly for the first time: "Welcome." The doorways pictured on the following pages—gracing homes from California to Connecticut—tell visitors that each owner is glad you came and that you are about to tour a much-loved garden.

Doorways may also give a clue to what lies ahead. Anne Coke's arrangement of potted plants foretells other locations where plants in pots will play a major role. The Greenwich doorway of Cecile McCaull and the Memphis entrance of Bonny Martin, both almost encircled with plant material, let you know that you will be walking through a garden of mature, interesting specimens.

The actual approach and entry into the garden proper may be through a gate or arbor, veiling the treasures that lie beyond and piquing one's curiosity at the same time. Such is the case with Holly Brigham's garden. Why an Asian moongate in St. Louis? There's a good reason, and visitors will learn some history on their tour of the garden.

Once inside, gates and arbors serve as dividers, announcing the passage from one garden room to the next, alerting the visitor to a change of pace, a shift in focus. In Lois Baylis's garden in Darien, Connecticut, a wooden gate marks the transition from manicured lawn to a raised walkway over a marsh.

Gates, doorways, and garden entrances might be compared to book jackets. The pictures and blurbs give you some indication as to what's inside, but you need to read the book—to walk through the garden—to get the whole picture. And, to pursue another book analogy, stepping through a garden gate is like passing through the wardrobe door in C. S. Lewis's *The Lion, the Witch and the Wardrobe*. Who knows what magic might lie on the other side?

previous page ❈ The long leaves of evergreen jasmine (*Jasmine armandii*) embrace the wrought-iron gates designed by sculptor Joseph Havel for this Houston, Texas, entrance. Other gates, leading visitors from one garden room to the next, echo the design element of the overlapping circles.

above ❈ The gilt grapes and leaves on this gate by Tulsa designer Ernest Weiman pay homage to the wine country setting of this Napa Valley, California, home, while the roses (lower right) give fortunate visitors a clue as to what lies just around the corner in Mary and Steven Read's garden.

right ❈ Brick columns with white capitals and a graceful wooden gate frame an avenue of pines, beeches, and maples lining the approach to the Langdon Farm home of Suzanne Whitmore on the Eastern Shore of Maryland.

above ❖ Easter lilies, hydrangeas, cineraria, geraniums, and marguerites add spring color to more long-lasting components—ivy topiaries and camellia standards—at Anne Coke's front door in the Preston Hollow section of Dallas, Texas.

left ❖ Visitors to Helen Hickingbotham's home in Hillsborough, California, pass by a bountiful variety of ferns, cyclamen, impatiens, and fringed bleeding heart before reaching the doorway.

overleaf, left ❖ Cecile McCaull believes the climbing hydrangea (*Hydrangea petiolaris*) that now encircles her Greenwich, Connecticut, doorway was probably planted shortly after the house was built in 1926. When she and her husband, Philip, moved here in 1975, she began encouraging it to go across the top of the doorway and then start down the other side. All was well until a workman "trimmed" it back to the first side. Then she started once again.

overleaf, right ❖ Magnolia and holly frame the door of Bonny and David Martin's home in Memphis, Tennessee. Asian plaques and horses offer a prelude to the Japanese-style garden and bonsai collection that lie ahead.

above My husband, Phil, and I had been talking about taking out all the Taxus (yews) in front of our house and replacing them with holly and boxwood. The deer were enjoying them, and in the winter the salt from the driveway when we had snow was turning them brown. But it was a big step; we were hesitant.

Rosemary Verey was coming to speak at the Garden Education Center and had asked to visit some Greenwich gardens. Ours was to be on her tour. I told Phil I was going to ask Rosemary Verey what she thought about taking the Taxus out.

When she arrived, the first thing I asked her when she got out of the car was whether we should keep the Taxus or take them out. She took one look at them and said, "If they were mine, I would have them out by tomorrow!"

They were gone by the end of the next day and have been replaced by boxwood and holly.

CECILE McCAULL, GREENWICH, CONNECTICUT

above ✿ Architectural plantstands stand out from, yet blend into, the color and style of this Shawnee Mission, Kansas, home. Norma Sutherland has filled them with the cool green of Christmas fern (*Polystichum acrostichoides*).

right ✿ Cymbidium orchids grace Gwen Babcock's front door in San Marino, California, echoing the red of the door and the red pots.

overleaf, left ✿ The arched opening in the nine-foot-high stone wall allows a glimpse of Colles Larkin's perennial border, but it reveals nothing of the real treasure—the 125 varieties of trees that John Larkin has planted in their Dellwood, Minnesota, garden. He has pushed the zone limits on many of them, especially the Japanese maples. One prize that "should not" survive the Zone-4 Minnesota winters is *Acer palmatum* 'Trompenburg', which is nevertheless doing very well after nine years.

overleaf, right ✿ An Asian-inspired moongate, crowned in Chinese wisteria (*Wisteria sinensis*), pays homage to the Chinese and Japanese exhibits that stood on this property during the 1904 St. Louis World's Fair. Old maps depict attractions called "Mysterious Asia" and "Fair Japan," where Holly Brigham now grows stands of bamboo and lovingly pampers a huge male gingko. Through the eye, or oculus, of the gate, visitors look down a walkway that accentuates rather than camouflages the narrowness of the 100-by-540-foot property.

A negative lightning bolt took out half of a 129-foot-long retaining wall that was nine feet high and over two feet thick. A huge twin-trunk cedar was clinging to the edge of the torn-away hillside. We decided to move it 150 feet across the garden. Workmen prepared a hole, and a 144-inch spade dug it up and carried it toward its new destination. Just before it was to be released, I decided it needed to be turned 180 degrees. One young, unbelieving workman looked at me in disbelief, then drawled, "Nooo problem, lady, it's your money!" Truth be told, I stopped cold for one millisecond, but then blurted out, "Turn it!" It was turned and lowered and some five or six guys conceded my point and got busy pushing in the dirt and watering. It took about three years and a lot of watering before the cedar, which was forty to sixty feet high, recuperated from its move and began to regain its former healthy presence. It's now been in its new location over ten years and appears quite happy.

COLLES LARKIN, DELLWOOD, MINNESOTA

Pleasures in my garden:

❀ *The majestic gingko after the first hard freeze when all the leaves come down, almost at once. You can hear them falling.*

❀ *On a crisp fall day the Acer japonicum 'Aconitifolium' is a blaze of orange, scarlet, peach, and yellow—a garden all by itself.*

❀ *The sound of the bamboo—rustling leaves and the occasional "clack" of the culms hitting each other.*

❀ *The smell of rosemary and thyme on my dog.*

HOLLY BRIGHAM, ST. LOUIS, MISSOURI

opposite Peace and tranquility. Those are the pleasures. Weeding the moss is almost like a meditation.

LOIS BAYLIS, DARIEN, CONNECTICUT

above ❖ An archway covered in Sally Holmes roses lures visitors from the carpark into Mary and Steven Read's garden. Named Read's Leap, with a nod to nearby Stag's Leap vineyards, this Napa Valley garden boasts more than fifty varieties of roses with several, including Sally Holmes, being repeated throughout to unify the property. Visitors' chances of seeing Sally Holmes in bloom are excellent, as it reblooms five or six times a season.

opposite ❖ This arbor gate in Lois Baylis's garden offers passage to a small island in the marshes off Darien, Connecticut, where visitors and weary gardeners can rest and view the changing moods of Long Island Sound.

2 Enjoy the View

SURELY ONE OF THE MAIN PLEASURES OF VISITING A HOME AND GARDEN IS TO experience the view that the owners enjoy every day, to see what they see when they are inside the house looking out, upstairs looking down, or stepping out onto the porch or patio. Russell Page in *The Education of a Gardener* (1994) says: "I prefer always to approach a private garden through the house. One of the qualities of a private garden lies just in the fact that it is private."

Views from the house drive the landscape design plan, whether by uncovering a nearby rock outcropping or enclosing a terrace so the neighbor's garage is not visible, or opening up a distant view of the sea or mountains. Prince Charles-Joseph de Ligne, a Belgian nobleman who counseled Marie Antoinette on her gardens, was asked to define "a fine view." His answer was that it is a joy forever, and that you can be sure you have one if you are continually going to the window.

In all but a few rare cases, the distant view will be a borrowed view. Few homeowners are able to own as far as the eye can see. (An exception might be Biltmore House, the Gilded Age estate of George W. Vanderbilt in Asheville, North Carolina, that overlooks 8,000 acres of managed forestland in the Appalachian foothills.) Although the word "borrowed" suggests taking or using something that isn't yours, borrowed landscape is a time-honored tradition. The term *shakkei* in Japan translates to "borrowed scenery" and was first mentioned in a Chinese gardening manual from the seventeenth century. Landscape designers James van Sweden and Wolfgang Oehme say they begin their assessment of a site in just that way, searching for surrounding views to feature as "borrowed scenery," whether they be distant hills, a body of water, or even major trees on a neighbor's property.

Anne and Gary Bradley had their contemporary home in Colorado Springs designed with a wall of windows overlooking the borrowed scenery of Pike's Peak and the Garden of the Gods. In small city gardens, the eye is brought close to the house by maximizing interest in the available space. In Lillian Balentine Law's garden a long, narrow pool underscores the rectilinear quality of the property, while a statue in a niche gives the eye a place to stop. Ten months of bloom—camellias begin at Christmas, white Snow azaleas follow in April, roses flower from May to Thanksgiving—sustains the focus on the enclosed garden.

The Daytons kept the interest inside the boundaries of their 100-by-170-foot Palm Beach lot by dividing it into four garden rooms—a shade garden, an herb garden, a palm allee, and a rose garden embellished with an intricate mosaic design of old brick. Even from the second-floor balcony, the eye is enticed down to the pattern; focus stays within the garden.

As we visit the next few gardens, we'll see some in which the nearby picture is eloquently developed to "keep you going to the window," even an upstairs window, and some in which the distant view of a tree or of borrowed scenery has been framed to achieve the maximum impact.

previous page ✣ From the sitting room, guests look out on a carpet of different kinds of thyme to a semicircle of shrub roses punctuated by an urn overflowing with annuals. Looking back toward the house is equally rewarding.

left ✣ The view from Lillian Balentine Law's breakfast nook is through the carefully pruned branches of a loropetalum (*Loropetalum chinense*). It frames an oasis of calm in a 75-by-200-foot lot just two blocks from a busy Atlanta thoroughfare. A slender reflecting pool bordered by 200 White Triumphator tulips leads to a brick wall that masks neighboring houses and the Laws' garage. The tulips were refrigerated, then planted in mid-January. "You can't plant them in the fall here," she explains. "They don't get enough cold." She confides that she had emptied the icemaker on them to hold the bloom until the photographer arrived.

above ✣ The view has changed for Lucy and Bill Reno, but not entirely. For thirty years they lived in a home whose previous owners had commissioned Thomas Church to design their property, including three of Church's signature decks off the house. When they moved to this townhome in the Carmel Valley of the Monterey Peninsula in central California, Bill had the Thomas Church deck reproduced. From their dining room, the Renos look out on an armillary sphere they bought in Sweden years ago. Lucy says this and other garden ornaments that have followed make them feel at home.

right ✣ A wall of glass opens onto this Pebble Beach property edged with 250 native California trees—cypress, sycamore, redwood, and coast live oak. Natives were chosen by owner and architect Lee von Hasseln because, once established, they will depend only on rainfall. Water shortages are a prime concern in the evolving garden design, so for her first three years Lee has concentrated on geophytes (bulbs, corms, tubers, rhizomes), many from South Africa, that have underground storage organs to withstand drought. White blossoms dominate, and the hummingbirds love them.

Lee has instituted so many conservation measures that "the water and electric meters spin backwards." Passive solar energy pours through the ¾-inch glass walls laminated with ultraviolet block, protecting eyes from cataract-causing rays and preventing fabrics from fading. At the winter solstice, sunlight extends sixteen feet into the house, warming the limestone floors.

Overleaf ✣ Henrietta Fridholm is no longer surprised to look out and find Mr. P., the neighborhood peacock, admiring his reflection in the picture window or strolling across her terrace that overlooks Lake St. Clair in Grosse Pointe, Michigan. He's been "around" more than two years, visiting select houses for cashews and sunflower seeds.

above ❖ The view from the raised main floor of
Carolands, the 1920s chateau in Hillsborough,
California, restored by Ann Johnson, focuses on a
parterre designed for the original garden by French
landscape artist Achille Duchêne, one of the few
elements actually implemented. British landscape
architect Martin Lane Fox incorporated the parterre
into his landscape design for the restored chateau.

opposite ❖ These intriguing patterns can best
be viewed from the balcony of Joanne and Alan
Dayton's Palm Beach, Florida, home. Warm-
colored bricks, in a pattern inspired by a Roman
mosaic floor, swirl around islands of clipped grass
and fruit trees in terracotta planters. Roses fill the
corner beds.

left ✣ John and Colles Larkin can enjoy the uninterrupted view of a lilac tree (*Syringa reticulata*) in full bloom in late June in their Dellwood, Minnesota, garden. Forty years ago, John tentatively cleared ten oaks from his under-two-acre property; then he toppled forty-one more, creating space for more than a hundred choice varieties of Japanese maples, regular and weeping katsuras, a Chinese white fringe tree, and a dawn redwood he has planted since then.

above ✣ Anne and Gary Bradley's contemporary house sits at an elevation of 6,800 feet on a golf course in Colorado Springs. Their never-to-be-obstructed view encompasses the red rocks and foothills of the Garden of the Gods and Pike's Peak on the horizon. Low plantings with minimal water needs ease the transition from house to garden but do not block the view.

overleaf, left ✣ The view from Tricia Saul's home on Chesapeake Bay looks past trees—maples, a yellowwood (*Cladrastis lutea*), and an Atlantic white cedar (*Chamaecyparis thyoides*)—from the original plantings a hundred years ago.

overleaf, right ✣ On pages 14 and 15, we passed through the gates to Langdon Farm, Suzanne Whitmore's house on the Eastern Shore of Maryland. This is the view we would see from the other side of the house, looking out to Harris Creek.

Gardening has opened my eyes to our environment. We're involved with the Chesapeake Bay Foundation, the Eastern Shore Land Conservation, and the John Smith Trail—organizations working to conserve our wonderful resources. We plant with birds, bees, and butterflies in mind. They are my flying, buzzing, flitting flowers!

TRICIA SAUL, EASTON, MARYLAND

We first saw Langdon Farm while sailing in the Chesapeake. One evening we anchored in Dun Cove on Harris Creek and we could see the house. I said to my husband, "It's so beautiful. I would love to live in a house just like this one some day!" We bought the property fourteen years ago. There are more pleasures than I can count:

* *30,000 daffodils blooming in the spring.*
* *A row of ornamental cherry trees in full bloom all day, every day, for ten days in early spring. A friend calls it Philosopher's Row.*
* *Making pickles with the very same friend from the cucumbers grown in the vegetable garden every summer for the last ten years. We call ourselves the Langdon Farm Picklers.*
* *Sitting on the dock, watching the red glow of a Chesapeake Bay sunset.*
* *Wondering about the people buried in our tiny cemetery.*
* *The absolute quiet of a winter morning when the garden is covered with snow.*

Of course, there are challenges. I hate it when the Japanese beetles arrive, when it is almost too hot to garden, when we plant a new row of lilacs and the one in the middle dies. But the pleasures far exceed the challenges. Little did I know the joy it would bring when we embarked on this project fourteen years ago.

SUZANNE WHITMORE, LANGDON FARM, SHERWOOD, MARYLAND

3 Let's Take a Walk

ONCE WE'VE ENTERED THE GARDEN AND ENJOYED THE VIEW, WHERE DO WE GO next? Steps, bridges, walkways, and paths guide our feet and our eyes to the next reward in the garden.

Steps, according to Thomas Church, are more than just a connection between two levels. In *Hard Surfaces* (1955) he said, "They can have strength and crispness of line. They can steady the composition, point the direction, and ornament the scene. . . .They can put you in a leisurely mood, make you hurry, or arouse your curiosity."

Much of Church's description of steps could apply to bridges, also. While a bridge is a connection between the two sides of a stream, it also underscores the style of the garden. A rustic stone across a brook is a subtle continuation of the path, reaffirming that this is a natural woodland garden, as it does in Louise Wrinkle's Birmingham garden. Or it can "ornament the scene" and signal a more dramatic shift, as it does in Mary Read's Napa garden.

Walkways and paths do all of the above and much more. Hugh Johnson in *Principles of Gardening* (1996) declared that no single element in the design of a garden is as important as where you put your paths. "Paths dictate," he said, "not just to the feet but to the mind, the route to follow, the points from which the planting will be seen, indeed the whole shape of the garden. They are . . . the track the eyes move on."

He adds, "Their business is to conduct you to all the best places, and it is just as well if they let you know when you have arrived by bringing you to a landmark—a seat or summer house or a view. Paths should live up to their promises."

Historically, the European approach to paths has been a straight line, such as those clearly drawn in the classic Italian and French gardens. An early garden authority, J. C. Loudon, stated the principle this way in *Encyclopedia of Gardening* (1822): "The principle of a sufficient reason should never be lost sight of in laying out walks . . . that is, no deviation from a straight line should ever appear, for which a reason is not given in the position of the ground, trees, or other accompanying objects."

In China and Japan, there was and is quite a different attitude toward paths. An early Chinese garden manual says that paths should "meander like playing cats." Marc Keane explains the "meandering" in *Japanese Garden Design* (1996): "Through careful design of the paths, the gardener controls not only the cadence of motion through a garden but what is seen as well. . . .Walking across uneven stepping stones (*tobi-ishi*), the guest is forced, by the precariousness of the footing, to look down and focus on the path. The designer has effectively stopped the guest from looking about at that time, but after a short run of stepping stones, the designer will invariably place a larger stone. . . . The larger surface of the stone allows the guest to stop comfortably, raise his head and look around at the garden. The designer has carefully chosen this spot for its view."

Steps, bridges, paved walkways, and paths all direct the visitor and the eye to another part of the garden, hurrying or slowing the step, piquing interest, being beautiful in their own right.

STEPS

previous page ✿ Stepping-stone faces by
Berkeley artist Marcia Donahue slow the pace
before the climb up the steps to the woodland
trail in Virginia Israelit's Portland, Oregon,
garden. The hydrangea blossoms gives visitors
another reason to pause.

right ✿ These steps, in the Carsons' Newtown
Square, Pennsylvania, garden, curve past a
Magnolia grandiflora espaliered against an ivy-
covered wall and join a path that leads to the
front door. The fox from Clayton Bright's *Fox and
Hound* sniffs its way along the stone wall at the
edge of the garden. (See page 217.)

overleaf, left ✿ This was a steep, oval
amphitheater until Virginia Israelit slid from the
top to the bottom on a rainy Portland, Oregon,
day. Her husband suggested steps, and her
landscape designer and friend Michael Schultz
designed the terracing you see here, edged with
the glow of variegated Hakone grass (*Hakonechloa
macra* 'Aureola'), a hosta collection, plumes from
Rodgersia pinnata superba, and the upright foliage
of *Iris pseudacorus*. The broad stairs promise
something grand at the top, and they deliver—
a vista of mountains and the Willamette River.

overleaf, right ✿ The fact that these steps are
less traveled make them all the more inviting.
Perhaps Bunny and Juan O'Callahan's secret
garden lies at the other end, nestled amongst the
seaside rocks and protected by a high stone wall
on their Stonington, Connecticut, property.

above *I had heard about this word "perennials," so I said to Michael Schultz, a young landscape designer, "Let's plant a few of those." That was in 1989; creating this one small area so I could have cut flowers for my office desk was like opening Pandora's box for me. I was hooked. Michael started introducing me to designers and nurserymen in the Northwest and ones who would travel to the area. I liked to cook, and they loved to eat. Dinner discussions were lively. They insisted that I learn the correct botanical names before they would talk to me about new plants and where I could get them. Many a night I would fall asleep with* The Royal Horticulture Encyclopedia *in bed with me. My husband asked if I thought I could learn the nomenclature by osmosis if I slept with the book on top of me.*

Recently, our whole family hauled sand in buckets to build the play area for our first grandchild. Upon its completion, we all sat in the sandbox with champagne to toast a good day's work. My son smiled and reminded me that not so many years ago I had yelled at him for knocking a croquet ball into my perennial border, but now thirty-six square feet of plants and shrubs could be decimated to make way for a one-year-old grandson's sandbox.

VIRGINIA ISRAELIT, PORTLAND, OREGON

❋ **above** *I feel wonder every day I am in my garden. In February I feel delight at the very first daffodils under a south window, get assurance that spring is near when the* Prunus *'Okame' lights up the lower garden, and sense my friends' satisfaction as they stop and stare at the front walk when it's awash in tulips for a month—my annual splurge. In the fall, we can't give away all the tomatoes, zucchini, beans, zinnias, and herbs that continue until the first frost. And in the winter I feel an extraordinary wonder once again, when leaves fall off the* Cornus *'Midwinter Fire' and their brilliant red and yellow stems illuminate the nearby* Mahonia aquifolium *and* Bergenia *'Bressingham Ruby' that turn from green to magenta with the first frost.*

GAY BARCLAY, POTOMAC, MARYLAND

opposite ❋ An Atlanta, Georgia, backyard built of a hundred truckloads of dirt as a setting for young sons' forts and games is now Kathy Hendricks's garden on three levels, showcasing collections of narcissus, magnolias, boxwoods, camellias, herbs, perennials, and eight different viburnums, including the thirty-year-old Chinese snowball (*Viburnum macrocephalum*) at the top of the stairs. It is entwined with the white climbing rose, *Rosa* 'Madame Alfred Carrière'.

above ❋ These steps lead guests down to a summer living area cut into a hillside in Gay Barclay's Potomac, Maryland, garden. As suburbia began surrounding their once-quiet farm, the Barclays created a "second home" away from the road, with living and dining areas, a well-equipped kitchen, a potting shed, and a vegetable garden. (See pages 73 and 246–47.)

❀ above *A natural woodland means we have lots of shade, but in the spring, ephemeral wildflowers sing their song before the bare trees leaf out.*

Not many people would tell you that winter is their favorite time of year. But the air is clear and clean, there are no leaves or colored flowers to distract you, and you can see the bones of the garden as well as the lichen on the trees.

LOUISE WRINKLE, BIRMINGHAM, ALABAMA

❀ opposite, above *We had an ice storm and then a "straight-line" wind, and were without power for thirteen days each time. We lost many old oaks. We learned nature cannot be tamed. We learned to adjust. One has no other choice.*

BICKIE McDONNELL, MEMPHIS, TENNESSEE

✿ Spring visitors who cross this year-round stream on the rough-hewn stone bridge are welcomed by Virginia bluebells (*Mertensia virginica*) edging the path in Louise Wrinkle's woodland garden in Birmingham, Alabama. Paths were an addition that Louise made when she and her husband moved back to her parents' home. "I could hike cross-country to anywhere in the woods," she said. "Now the garden is accessible and pleasant for other people too."

above ✿ Bickie and Mike McDonnell's three-acre garden in Memphis, Tennessee, has been described as a "smorgasbord of sensory pleasure . . . but always there is a sense of refinement." That's certainly true of this arched bridge that leads to a shady area of native azaleas, wild blue phlox, woodpoppies, foamflowers, and dogwood.

left ✿ A footbridge of Vermont granite spans a stream and marks the passage from the rhododendron garden into the flowering shrub walk in Gayle Maloney's Bernardsville, New Jersey, garden.

overleaf ✿ A daughter's wedding was excuse enough to install this Giverny-inspired bridge over the pool in Sue McKinley's Mediterranean-style garden in Montecito, California.

WALKWAYS

top ✲ This walkway edges a hill overlooking the San Gabriel Valley in San Marino, California. Gwen Babcock, who gardens from an electric wheelchair, put in this section first, then extended it to loop back up to the house at the far end. She said, "A path should go someplace, not require you to turn around and come back the same way." Jointly designed by a landscape architect and a structural engineer, it is heavily reinforced with steel bars. Gwen's daughter says, "When the next California earthquake takes the rest of the hill away, this walkway will still be standing, like a great overpass in the sky."

bottom ✲ A walkway reflecting the soft tones of their contemporary home flows through Anne and Gary Bradley's gated courtyard garden. The plantings, planned as a complement to the architecture and the Bradleys' art collection, and inspired by the artist Henri Matisse, "create an expressive collage of startling colors, forms, and shapes." Water is always a concern in Colorado Springs, so they have xeriscaped here and in other areas. Plantings are safe from deer, rabbits, and dogs, but the Bradleys report there's still an army waiting to attack—voles, magpies, gophers, slugs, aphids, and harlequin bugs.

opposite ✲ Mary Stanley's walkway in Dellwood, Minnesota, meanders above the woodland wildflowers that she has been planting and encouraging for twenty years. In the foreground circle is wild ginger (*Asarum europaeum*). The next section features white trillium, and the large leaves of mayapples (*Podophyllum peltatum*) can be seen in the distance.

overleaf, left ✲ Japanese wisteria (*Wisteria floribunda*) shades cymbidium orchids and ferns on this entry walk to the home of Berenice Spalding in Hillsborough, California. At the end is a Japanese maple and a water garden in an antique Thai container. The house, designed by architect Joseph Esherick, was built in 1963.

overleaf, right ✲ The curve of the walkway is echoed by the curve of the arbor's arches in Paula Soholt's St. Paul, Minnesota, garden. Known as "the Monet walkway," it offers, according to Paula, "a riotous display—vines twine, roses climb, and fruits glisten on the espaliered trees." Tunnel arbors were popular in Renaissance gardens and had their own renaissance in nineteenth- and early twentieth-century gardens in England—and at Claude Monet's Giverny.

🌸 above *My love of gardening has been inspired by fellow gardeners, many of whom continue to be stalwart mentors in all things horticultural. Hands-on propagating workshops have forced me to build a plant nursery—what a joy! Plants from the nursery travel to new places in the gardens of friends and passersby.*

The tree peony collection is the signature of our spring garden. Tree peonies were somewhat unknown and untested in our Zone-4 gardens ten years ago when we first planted them. Today, these sixty or so trees are showstoppers when in bloom. I look forward to cutting the ten-inch blossoms for floating floral displays and to sharing bouquets with special friends.

PAULA SOHOLT, ST. PAUL, MINNESOTA

above ✣ This arbor of thirty-two tricolored European beech trees (*Fagus sylvatica* 'Roseomarginata') is aglow with color all summer long in Elizabeth and William Martin's garden in Essexville, Michigan.

right ✣ An arbored walkway leads to the *potager* at Carolands, the Hillsborough, California, chateau and gardens recently restored by Ann Johnson. Climbing Cecile Brunner roses already cover the arches.

overleaf ✣ Under the gourd walk! Dipper gourds and an occasional snake gourd invite birds to set up housekeeping in this trellised walkway in Gayle Maloney's garden in Bernardsville, New Jersey. House wrens accept the invitation and help control the slug population. *Clematis* 'Ernest Markham' and Awakening roses and climbing Cecile Brunner roses offer shade and protection.

above ✿ Stones, laid with the recommended randomness of a Japanese garden, keep visitors watching where they step in Lois Baylis's Darien, Connecticut, garden. The path starts at the edge of the entrance driveway and leads visitors over a hill to hidden gardens near the house—a grass garden, a sunken garden, and a contemplation garden.

right ✿ Here's a path with a history. It leads through a rockery, first established on actual bedrock in the 1920s, uncovered and resuscitated by Susan Stevenson, the current owner of High Hatch in Portland, Oregon. Earlier owners, the Kerr family, shipped grain to the Orient and used stones from China as ballast on the return trip. The stones were then used to pave a path through the rock garden.

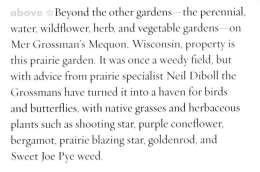

above ✳ Beyond the other gardens—the perennial, water, wildflower, herb, and vegetable gardens—on Mer Grossman's Mequon, Wisconsin, property is this prairie garden. It was once a weedy field, but with advice from prairie specialist Neil Diboll the Grossmans have turned it into a haven for birds and butterflies, with native grasses and herbaceous plants such as shooting star, purple coneflower, bergamot, prairie blazing star, goldenrod, and Sweet Joe Pye weed.

left ✳ It would be hard to navigate your way through Leland Miyano's garden in Kahalu'u on Oahu, Hawaii, without this well-defined path. When Leland bought the property twenty-five years ago, it was a one-acre flat, suburban lawn. Now cycads, aroids, and native Hawaiian plants fill the ground and cling to tree branches and trunks. (See page 205.) Many of the plants were collected when Miyano worked with Brazilian artist Roberto Burle Marx and botanical artist Margaret Mee in rescuing plants in ecosystems being clear-cut in South America.

above ✿ Autumn light illuminates the tassels on fountain grass (*Pennisetum alopecuroides*) lining a path at Brigham Hill Farm, Shirley and Peter Williams's home in Grafton, Massachusetts. The path marks the line where highly developed gardens—perennial, herb, vegetable, cutting—give way to a field of milkweed and New England aster.

opposite ✿ A split-rail fence lines the grassy lane to an 1850 Tennessee cantilevered log barn saved from demolition by Pat and Carl Hartrampf. The barn was disassembled in Tennessee, then painstakingly restored at Winfield, their 200-acre working farm in Highlands, North Carolina. It is one of two salvaged historic buildings on the farm; the other is an 1828 log house from Georgia.

✽ opposite *One beautiful fall day in October, we had some friends to lunch. They brought a houseguest, a Tahitian princess. We have never been to Tahiti, but we think of it as probably the world's most beautiful place. After lunch we walked around the garden. The princess lagged behind and was gazing up at the sky. We went back to see what she was watching. She was standing under a massive old sugar maple. The sky was bright blue and the sugar maple leaves were fluttering quietly down, blazing scarlet, orange, and clear yellow against the sky. She turned to us and exclaimed, "I have never seen anything so beautiful in my life!"*

We've never looked at our garden in quite the same way since.

SHIRLEY WILLIAMS, BRIGHAM HILL FARM, GRAFTON, MASSACHUSETTS

✽ above *Glimpsed for the first time spilling across a high plateau of 4,000 feet in the southern Appalachian Mountains, the farm had "adventure" written all over it, beckoning to us like a siren. Almost twenty years later, we are still smitten.*

The grandchildren have been our constant inspiration and coconspirators in this adventure, full participants in the good and sometimes painful experiences. Learning which are the good snakes and how to identify ginseng in the woods, mucking out the barn, gathering eggs, exercising the horses, catching a swarm of bees, or rounding up stray cattle—they were always brimming with enthusiasm. Six are now in college, and the younger two are juniors in high school. This summer, all managed to sandwich in a few days on the farm between trips to Europe, India, and Habitat [for Humanity] building in New Orleans.

We are often asked, "Well, what do you raise on this farm?" And the answer is always the same: "Grandchildren!"

PAT HARTRAMPF, WINFIELD FARM, HIGHLANDS, NORTH CAROLINA

4 There Are Places to Pause

WHETHER CLOSE BY THE HOUSE, AS A DELIGHTFUL DESTINATION, OR SIMPLY AS A punctuation mark along the visitor's path, a place to pause plays a major role in a garden's design. Close by, it is really an extension of the house, another room that may be known as a porch, loggia, patio, terrace, or veranda. It reflects our desire, our need to be outside when temperature and weather permit and to merge the house and the garden into an artistic whole.

Thomas Church, writing in the 1950s, articulated in *Gardens Are for People* what we now take for granted: "There are a number of phrases in use which express in general terms our longing to live *in* our site, such as 'the integration of the house and garden,' 'indoor-outdoor living,' and 'the relation of shelter to land.'. . . It is not a new idea. The Egyptians planned their house and gardens together. The Romans knew all about it. The Greeks had a word for it; and the Renaissance Italians developed it to a fine art. They had outside living rooms, dining rooms, corridors, and entrance halls. . . . The terrace, in all periods of gardening, and whether called *atrium*, *close*, *promenade*, or *lanai*, has been an obviously man-made part of the garden. . . . Today the 'terrace' area is for outdoor living."

A second kind of place to pause is set apart from the house but sited to best enjoy the breezes and beauty of the garden. These shelters might take the form of a pergola, gazebo, pavilion, belvedere, pagoda, teahouse, poolside cabana, or even an orangery designed for al fresco dining and entertaining.

Thomas Church advocated a terrace far enough away so that the view back to the house is pleasant. Decks became his signature, and he said that they, too, had historical precedent. "The wooden balconies of eighteenth-century European design were forerunners, and the spacious front porches and verandas of English and American architecture during the Victorian era were ancestors. But porches have become detached from houses and wander freely around the property—sometimes jutting out over it. . . . These wandering porches . . . are now what we call decks." Gwen Babcock's deck is a case in point, providing a "room" that hangs over the fault line that marks the edge of her garden. The coast live oak that shelters the spot would qualify as "living sculpture" by Church's definition.

Seats or benches, carefully sited throughout the garden, offer another means of rest for the visitor's weary feet. In the overall landscape design, though, they do much more. They offer the eye places to pause as it sweeps over the garden. They are, depending on their placement and style, the comma, the period or— if commanding in design or color—the exclamation point in the garden. They present a restful interlude to the expanses of lawn, the borders of flowers. They help anchor the garden under its canopy of trees. And they can be objets d'art, garden ornaments in their own right.

These places to pause often have stories to tell—their origin or inspiration, their age, even how often they are used. A fine old bench covered with lichen may suggest a serious gardener—who doesn't take time to sit. On our garden tour, we'll begin near the house, move out to places designed for entertaining and relaxing, then see how garden seats contribute to the garden's design and mystique.

✻ **above** *I think my love of gardening came to me through osmosis; I didn't know it was happening. When I was a tiny child, my mother made ravishing arrangements from flowers grown by my father in our gardens in Little Compton, Rhode Island. Canterbury bells, roses, and delphiniums dominated. In the vegetable garden, huge lush dahlias grew along with herbs (tarragon being my father's favorite) and vegetables. Our tomatoes were spectacular. But often there was an equally spectacular fat horned tomato worm present, alongside a large black spider who wove a complicated web with a zigzag pattern etched in it. Both terrified me.*

PENELOPE HARRIS, WYNDMOOR, PENNSYLVANIA

✻ **opposite** *Once I realized that roses worked magnificently planted with my perennials, my life changed. I always loved roses, and when I added them into my borders, the garden developed a bosom that spilled over itself with texture, color, and fragrance.*

The winter of 2004 was devastatingly cold. I lost so many long-established English roses and the magnificent Paul's Himalayan Musk rose that covered my trellis. The devastation that occurred to plants that I had nurtured and brought to maturity caused me such grief. I have been replanting, but just as a new puppy is fine, an old and trusted ally is irreplaceable.

PAULINE RUNKLE, THE GARDEN AT THREE PLUM HILL, MANCHESTER-BY-THE-SEA, MASSACHUSETTS

previous page ✿ Cecile and Philip McCaull's flagstone terrace in Greenwich, Connecticut, is truly an extension of their English manor-style house and an introduction to the beautifully restored and expanded garden that lies beyond. The McCaulls have lived in this house, built in 1925, for more than thirty years, and theirs was one of the first gardens in the East to be featured on the Garden Conservancy's Open Days.

opposite ✿ Two enormous eighty-year-old Japanese cherry trees (*Prunus subhirtella* 'Pendula') offer cool, green shelter from the hot summer sun on Penelope Harris's flagstone terrace in Wyndmoor, Pennsylvania. In April, their blossoms form a glorious pink tent.

above ✿ Climbing roses blur the line between house and garden in Pauline Runkle's flowering masterpiece in Manchester-by-the-Sea, Massachusetts. Two teak chairs and a table offer a respite from deadheading, weeding, transplanting, and from cutting roses, perennials, annuals, and dramatic foliage for her signature flower arrangements.

overleaf, left ✿ When Sigourney Cheek added a master bedroom to their 1929 Tudor-style house in Nashville, Tennessee, she also added a trellised porch. It is here she sits each summer morning, watching the abundant bird life and enjoying the ever-evolving work of art that is her garden. A sculpture major when she was in college, she has placed round boxwood at the ends of beds and dramatic pyramidal trees at key points along the serpentine brick wall that encloses two sides of the corner property.

overleaf, right ✿ Just a few steps from Mary and Steven Read's California house is this rose-shaded pergola, an invitation to come outside and enjoy the idyllic Napa Valley weather. Pink Sparrieshoop and white Sombreuil roses emerge from openings in the Idaho slate floor to embrace the supporting columns. Star jasmine was originally used to shade the area, but its vigorous growth hid the graceful lines of the columns.

opposite *When we moved into our home thirty years ago, there was no garden. For the first two years I would consult with a wonderful woman who lived next door and had a lush flower garden. Just when we were seriously improving our landscaping, the woman moved. The next owner was not interested in gardening, and one day I noticed a large bulldozer arriving to dig a hole for a swimming pool. I rushed over and asked what she planned to do with the flowers in the garden. It was early spring and most of the perennials were barely showing. She told me she didn't plan to save any of them. I asked if she'd mind if I dug up the flowers. She was happy to give me anything I could take before the bulldozer did its worst. I was young in those days and spent the next three days digging and digging.*

This spring, the original woman's granddaughter moved into a new house with a perfect space to start a perennial garden. As a wedding gift I took her "offspring" of all the plants I had retrieved from her grandmother's garden: a wonderful wine-red bearded iris, blue Siberian iris, blue lady bells (Adenaphora)—which I have never seen in a garden center—Wedgwood blue Japanese roof iris, blue ornamental thistles, and white Love in a Mist (Nigella).

SIGOURNEY CHEEK, NASHVILLE, TENNESSEE

above *My love of decorating our home always made me want to have the inside and the outside flow together. My children say they remember being in a playpen too long sometimes while I became lost in my gardening and its pleasures.*

My garden is a passion that embraces me whenever I enter it, and there is an inner peace I find immediately. I adore seeing the garden mature, and I love to update the plants and find new and unusual plant material. We say each year we think the garden is its prettiest. This may be our passion and the maturing process coming together.

MARY READ, READ'S LEAP, NAPA, CALIFORNIA

❀ opposite *My grandmother and my great-aunt were both great gardeners. I remember my great-aunt, who was a landscape gardener, coming to visit us and unpacking more plants than clothes from her suitcases. They helped my mother lay out her gardens on our farm in Indiana and taught me the name of every bird and flower. I feel their influence all the time, especially around the compost heap. They were organic gardeners and, like them, I have never used a spray of any kind on this place, neither to kill insects nor enhance growth.*

Over sixty years ago, in 1947, my grandmother, Mrs. Robert Scott Spilman, wrote a wonderful piece on composting for The Garden Club of America Bulletin titled "An Organic Gardener States the Case for Humus."

GAY BARCLAY, POTOMAC, MARYLAND

opposite ✻ The Barclays bought their five-acre farm in Potomac, Maryland, twenty-five years ago, and for the first fifteen years could not see a light from another house in any direction. Then Washington's suburbia moved in, and Gay Barclay moved out, in a sense. She set to work 200 yards from the house, cutting into the sloping terrain behind on old corncrib and installing a stone retaining wall. Now there is the summer "living room," pictured here, a dining room nearby, and a summer kitchen next to her vegetable garden. (See pages 246–47.)

above ✻ Crossbeams and nearby trees cast shadows on the floor of this pergola in an Illinois garden. The surrounding garden simply continues through the structure, with pots and hanging baskets of fuchsia carrying the color and inviting hummingbirds to call.

above ✢ Wisteria vine adds to the sculptural strength of this elegant pergola in a Houston garden. When the wisteria has finished, other vines take over the blooming—climbing roses (*Rosa* 'Buff Beauty,' *R.* 'Mermaid,' *R.* 'Sombreuil'), trumpet vine (*Campsis grandiflora*), clematis (*Clematis* 'Miss Bateman'), monkey's comb vine (*Pithecoctenium crucigerum*), and—pictured here— yellow passionflower (*Passiflora citrina*). The bronze table base and stools, shaped to resemble wood, are designed by sculptor Joseph Havel.

right ✢ In her San Marino, California, garden, filled with enticing destinations and places to pause, Gwen Babcock says that this deck under an old coast live oak has to be her favorite. A breeze rises from the San Gabriel Valley; Lacy Park, with its beautiful green canopy of trees, is just below. Every Fourth of July the Babcocks welcome almost 400 friends and family, half of them under four feet tall, to enjoy the fireworks set off in Lacy Park. Ten other fireworks displays are visible across the valley.

overleaf ✢ An orangery in Bettie Bearden Pardee's Newport, Rhode Island, garden does double duty. In the spring, when the tulips and cherry trees (*Prunus* x 'Hally Jolivette') are flowering, it may be the scene of an intimate dinner; in the winter, it may house pots of citrus. A dovecote on the edge of the property echoes the French architecture and stores garden equipment in fine style.

GARDEN SEATS

above ❖ A semicircular driveway at Judy and Charles Tate's home in Houston leads to a brick-and-wrought-iron entry pavilion, a nod to the architecture of their fifty-year-old New Orleans–inspired house. Birds-of-paradise plantings (*Strelitzia reginae*) flank the custom-designed bench, and creeping fig (*Ficus pumila*) is framed behind it.

right ❖ The rustic furniture and gazebo frame speak to a sense of place—the mountains of Highlands, North Carolina. Jenny Lynn Bradley loves the temperate rain-forest ecosystem in this summer garden. At 4,000 feet and with eighty inches of rain a year, she can grow peonies, lilacs, delphinium, dahlias, and the hostas and black-eyed Susans pictured here, which would not survive the heat in her Savannah garden.

opposite ❧ A delicate white, wrought-iron bench is outlined against bold tropical foliage, providing a place for the eye to pause and the visitor to rest in Meredith Marshall's Palm Beach, Florida, garden.

above ❧ Both the color and form of this garden bench catch the eye and invite the visitor to sit and enjoy the perennials in Margaret Weatherly Hall's garden in Prairie Village, Kansas. The garden, in a suburb of Kansas City, Missouri, that was once a treeless prairie on the Santa Fe Trail, is home to more than 5,000 bulbs, six different kinds of magnolias, and twenty-five varieties of peonies, as well as ten cultivars of boxwood—perhaps the biggest challenge when the late-winter winds come whistling across the prairie.

left ❧ A garden seat beckons across a wide expanse of lawn punctuated with mature trees. This Portland, Oregon, garden was developed over a period of fifty years by the previous owner; now Susan Bates has added her touch—"unusual plants, lots of 'drifts of one color,' tied together with greens and golds." Often open for garden tours, it was recently visited by the Rhododendron, Camellia and Magnolia Group of the Royal Horticultural Society.

left ✤ The graceful curve of this bench acts as a "comma," slowing the visitor's glance long enough to allow contemplation of the interplay of color and texture in this Chicago-area garden.

above ✤ Broad-leaved hostas embrace this bench in Bob and Marilyn Asplundh's garden in Bryn Athyn, Pennsylvania. Visitors might wonder which came first, the curved bench or the meticulously edged lawn; one certainly complements the other.

83

5 Ways With Water

WATER AS A GARDEN ELEMENT HAS A MAGICAL QUALITY UNEQUALED BY ANY OTHER. In this chapter we will "tour" gardens in which water's magic is creatively harnessed, beginning with those fortunate enough to border oceans or encompass large bodies of water. Then we'll move on to gardens that incorporate ponds and streams and, when none of these natural sources are available, use pools, even swimming pools, to introduce the sound and sight of water into the garden. Unusual fountains, a water garden in pots, a birdbath, and a "water table" will conclude our look at innovative ways with water.

The use of pools and fountains in gardens goes back to the earliest known gardens. Persian gardens were distinguished by narrow water features known as *chahar bagh*, rills that intersected at a pool in the center and divided the garden into quarters. The four rills represented the four rivers in the garden of Paradise. Influences of this early design are evident in the Taj Mahal gardens, in Muslim gardens as far east as Spain's Alhambra and Generalife, and in Italian Renaissance gardens. Noted French landscape architect André Le Nôtre repeated the theme in the seventeenth century in the canals he designed at Versailles.

England, too, embraced formal pools and fountains until Lancelot "Capability" Brown came along. Brown introduced naturalistic landscaping to landowners whose estates had been vastly enlarged by an act of Parliament. In the eighteenth century, millions of acres of public land in England were enclosed into private estates. The owners of this windfall embraced Brown's concept of offering sweeping vistas and making the grounds appear natural—smooth, undulating lawn rolling from the house out to clumps and belts of trees and to the essential element, a serpentine lake created by damming a river or stream on the property. Brown's style was praised for "perfecting nature" and damned for tearing out perfectly beautiful formal gardens. In the British journal *Garden History* (Summer 2001) there is an account of a conversation between Brown and the writer Hannah More. Brown explains his style in writer's terms: "Now *there*," pointing a finger, "I make a comma, and there," pointing to another spot, "where a more decided turn is proper, I make a colon; at another part, where an interruption is desirable to break the view, a parenthesis; now a full stop, and then I begin another subject." The lake, the water feature, was no doubt the full stop.

Water in Japanese gardens has an even more ancient history, and its varied and imaginative usage encompasses lakes and rivers, streams and pools, when space and topography permit. In the smallest of gardens a *tsukubai*—a simple basin catching water from a bamboo pipe—suffices.

A further refinement in the Japanese garden is the *suggestion* of water, achieved by raked sand in the *karesansui* or dry landscape garden developed by Zen Buddhist priests. In a later chapter we'll see how designer Isabelle Greene achieved this concept in Carol Valentine's garden in Santa Barbara, California. But for now, our tour takes us from gardens along Long Island Sound to gardens on North Carolina mountaintops; from Maine to Hawaii, with many stops along the route. In each garden, we will see how the designer made the most of the ocean, lake, pond, or stream that was a natural part of the property and how, when none was available, an innovative way was devised to introduce this essential ingredient into the garden's design.

previous page ✢ Close to the seashore but seemingly miles away is this pond in Bunny and Juan O'Callahan's Stonington, Connecticut, garden. Yellow irises (*Iris pseudacorus* 'Golden Nugget') light up the edge, and a Giverny-inspired bridge marks where the overflow begins its descent to the sea. A seasonal pond was dug out and lined with vinyl—three times. Bunny says, "Little did we know how hard it is to maintain a leakproof pool. I'm thinking a marsh might be better suited."

right ✢ Sitting on top of the world is this spring-fed pond on the Southern Highlands Reserve in Lake Toxaway, North Carolina. Betty and Robert Balentine (Lillian Balentine Law's son from her first marriage) call it home when they're not in Atlanta. Natives—Joe Pye Weed, wild hydrangeas, black-eyed Susans, dog hobble, rhododendron, and viburnum—circle the pond.

overleaf, left ✢ Not far away, near Highlands, North Carolina, is this lake on Winfield Farm. Atlanta residents Pat and Carl Hartramph have had no trouble luring grandchildren to spend summers down on the farm. Part of the attraction might be the menagerie of rare breeds—Scottish Highland cattle, Red Devon working oxen, Ramboulet sheep, Cashmere goats, llamas, Dalmatian dogs, Pygmy pigs, horses, and, yes, barn cats—and the occasional bear!

overleaf, right ✢ Cat mint (*Nepeta* 'Six Hill Giant') creates a wave of its own in the Stonington, Connecticut, garden of Bunny and Juan O'Callahan. On a peninsula jutting into Little Narragansett Bay and overlooking the island of Sandy Point, half of the eleven-acre property has been deeded to conservation and preservation. Visitors on the Garden Conservancy's Open Days can enjoy the remainder, what Bunny describes as "a relaxed sort of English garden, with plants popping up here and there where they seed."

opposite The Winfield Farm Solution to the Japanese Beetle Problem:

❀ *One paper Solo cup with two inches of water in it*

❀ *A flock of chickens*

❀ *A willing grandchild or other cheap labor*

Early in the morning (Japanese beetles are notoriously late sleepers), simply slip the cup under the beetle on the branch and tap the branch. Beetle falls in and cannot fly out because of the water. When you have a good number of beetles in the cup, race to the chickens—this is where the fun begins. Fling water and beetles into the midst of the chickens and stand back!

The perfect solution: No more beetles, no chemicals, happy gardener, happy chickens, and hilarious entertainment for the children! (If you do not have a flock of hens handy, simply flush down the toilet.)

PAT HARTRAMPF, WINFIELD FARM, HIGHLANDS, NORTH CAROLINA

above There is nothing quite like digging in the garden to relax and rejuvenate me. Even headaches can disappear when I'm gardening! I think there is something about digging in the earth that brings me back to nature and also helps me to feel, just a little, like I am assisting in God's beauty around us.

In the winter months, we get strong, icy winds that would make your eyes water and freeze. Still, it is very beautiful to watch the saltwater freeze in wave forms in the shallow waters while the swans come from their sheltered spots to seek food in the open waters.

BUNNY O'CALLAHAN, STONINGTON, CONNECTICUT

89

top ❋ A Japanese garden installed in the 1920s encircles this Portland, Oregon, pond. When Jill Josselyn Scheer and her husband moved here fifteen years ago, the pond was in such disrepair that all the rocks and plants had to be removed. After the restoration, the stepping stones were reinstalled and forty Japanese maples of various shapes and growth habits—and with such wonderful cultivar names as 'Bloodgood', 'Butterfly', 'Hupp's Dwarf', and 'Peaches and Cream'—were planted near the pond.

bottom ❋ A brook, edged with stone and planted with *Phlox divaricata* and other natives, meanders through Lee Petty's Chevy Chase, Maryland, garden.

opposite ❋ When the basement of the barn in the background was dug out, water from a deep aquifer was diverted into this prefabricated pond in Mary and Steven Read's Napa, California, garden. The center is sixteen feet deep, but a four-foot shelf around the edge makes it possible to plant containers of grasses and reeds to soften the edge. A swath of white valerian on the shore is cut back in June and blooms again in the fall. Water from the pond is used to irrigate the adjoining cottage garden.

left ✣ A cruciform pool is part of the architectural bones of Judy and Charles Tate's garden. Coated in dark plaster, it reflects views of the garden while water quietly disappears over the flagstone vanishing edge. Four stone pads hold low bowls of palm trees, indicative of Houston's semitropical environment. Beyond the pool, and reflected in it, is an antique brick wall inset with fig ivy. The wall frames a sculpture by Colombian artist Fernando Botero and conceals a functional shed beyond.

above ✣ In Helen Hickingbotham's garden in Hillsborough, California, a waterfall fills a hot tub, then spills over boulders into the swimming pool. Thomas Church designed the original garden when the couple moved here in 1940. He returned over the years to add areas and lay out paths that move visitors through the extensive gardens—past perennial beds and the secret garden, to the rose and vegetable gardens, then by the pool area to a composting yard, into a shade garden, by the owner's studio, lath houses, and a greenhouse— finally returning to the entrance courtyard.

🌸 above right *I worked for years as a professional photographer, and early morning is my favorite time to be out with my camera. One of my favorite moments was watching a sleepy bee wake up inside a flower. His furry body was laden with pollen and, as the morning sun warmed the blossom, he stretched, shook himself off, and then flew away in search of breakfast.*

SARAH HOOD SALOMON, BETHESDA, MARYLAND

🌸 opposite *On garden tours and in travels, I often see gardens far more sophisticated, more perfect, and more "designed," but that doesn't diminish my garden in my eyes. I am never bored or despondent in the garden. There is always something to weed, to move, to admire. And now that I have my first dog—a gorgeous black male standard poodle—to assist me when gardening, my life outdoors has a new, exuberant quality. Always changing, always a passion—that's a garden.*

SUSAN DEEKS, NEW VERNON, NEW JERSEY

above left ✿ After passing under a wisteria arbor at the front door, visitors to High Hatch, Susan Stevenson's home in Portland, Oregon, arrive at a courtyard with this formal brick pool. Star magnolia and white camellia shelter the cherub at the end.

above right ✿ A small stream of water flows from the lion's head fountain into a moss-covered basin in the Bethesda, Maryland, garden of Sarah and Robert Salomon, then overflows into the fishpond below. When the Salomons were first married they went house hunting in Robert's mind, but yard hunting in Sarah's. Both seem satisfied. They named their place ReveroF—*forever* spelled backward.

opposite ✿ This tiny pool sits atop a flourishing rock garden in Susan Deeks's landscape in New Vernon, New Jersey.

opposite ✿ A tiny jet of water breaks the surface of this pool in Joanne and Alan Dayton's garden in Palm Beach, Florida. The arc of the pool is repeated in the fragrant jasmine arbor and the inviting bench at the end.

above ✿ A fountain is the focal point of this courtyard planted by Lorelei Gibson as a green room, an extension of the 1930 house in the residential garden community of Mission Hills, Kansas. Three brick paths lead from the fountain into a sculpture garden, another courtyard centered by a wellhead, and through a teahouse to a perennial garden.

left ✿ The fountain holds its own against the backdrop of Lake St. Clair in Jane Manoogian's garden in Grosse Pointe, Michigan.

overleaf, left ✿ A sheet of water, its flow barely perceptible, covers a millstone, half sunk into the ground where three paths converge in Louise Wrinkle's Birmingham, Alabama, garden. The paths lead visitors through a woodland garden rich with native plants that are sometimes paired with their Asian counterparts.

overleaf, right ✿ On Oahu, Hawaii, but high in the hills and far from the ocean, Claire Johnson creates a garden of water lilies (*Nymphaea*) in glazed ceramic planters. Potted in dense, dark red soil, they are placed on bricks so the leaves float on the surface, the blooms rising above. Aquatic pond tabs and fish supply nutrients. At the edge of the lawn a border of Hawaiian ginger curves in front of a jacaranda tree in bloom. The cool breezes and heavy rainfall create a tropical paradise with, as Claire says, very few surprises.

above The garden is located in a suburb of Birmingham, in an Alabama woodland of towering pines and hardwoods, with changing topography and a small spring-fed stream at the rear. I grew up here and moved back in 1987 after my parents died.

At first I thought I wanted to stick to strictly native plants. When I realized how parallel the rich faunas of the southeast United States and that of the Orient are, I began to add oriental counterparts to their native cousins. For example, the native fringe tree (Chionanthus virginiana) *has an Oriental cousin (Chionanthus retusus).*

I have focused on some plant families—anything in the holly family (Aquifoliacaea), *the ranunculus family, and Ericaceae, a family that includes tiny heaths and tall rhododendrons and dozens of plants in between.*

LOUISE WRINKLE, BIRMINGHAM, ALABAMA

We were especially fortunate to receive advice from the late Edgar Denison. He was a botanist, published Missouri Wildflowers, and was an active volunteer at the Missouri Botanical Garden. After he divided his plants in the spring, he would pot the extras and put them out on the street with a sign that said "Take me and give me a home."

One of our favorites in the garden is a golden larch, Pseudolarix amabilis, grown from a seedling that was a gift from Edgar. He had grown several of these seedlings from a tree that hung over a neighbor's fence. The tree had come from the Chinese exhibit at the 1904 St. Louis World's Fair. The species was originally discovered by Robert Fortune, an explorer for the Royal Horticultural Society, in the mid-1800s. Fortune sent seedlings and some rooted cuttings back to England in sealed Wardian cases lashed to the masts of sailing ships, up out of the reach of the damaging salt spray. Isn't that an amazing story!

MARY OTT, ST. LOUIS, MISSOURI

opposite ❖ Placed near a much-used screened porch, this fountain in Mary and Tom Ott's St. Louis, Missouri, garden is made from sponge rock found on a farm south of St. Louis and drilled by sculptor Bob Cassily. A border of the shrub rose Carefree Beauty and blue agapanthus blocks a view of the nearby driveway.

above ❖ A "water table" on the Otts' terrace is a favorite for birds. The base of an old iron stove was fitted with a copper insert that now holds a collection of petrified wood and colorful stones that glisten in the water. A glass top quickly converts it from birdbath to coffee table. Hardy begonias lend a tropical flavor, as does the staghorn fern on the tree. In winter, the fern finds shelter in the greenhouse that holds Tom's collection of more than 500 orchids.

6 Borders, Beds, and Much, Much More

FOR MANY A GARDENER, PERENNIAL BORDERS SUCH AS THE ONES PICTURED HERE are a dream come true, a decades-long ambition realized. A glorious herbaceous border tells the visitor that here is an exceptional gardener, one who is knowledgeable in horticulture, surely, but also an artist—one who paints with plants.

Much of our passion to create the perfect border can be traced to two late nineteenth-century British figures—William Robinson and Gertrude Jekyll—and the English gardens that still show their influence. Robinson opposed the Victorian fashion of bedding out with brightly colored tender plants—red salvias, blue lobelias—which were brought along in heated glasshouses and then planted in masses, often forming a design such as a clock or the name of a town. He advocated an informal style of gardening with hardy species and even British wildflowers, and he was in a position to influence the taste of his contemporaries through his books and periodicals, *The Garden* and *Gardening Illustrated*.

Gertrude Jekyll, at about the same time, was an artist with horticultural expertise. Her flowing borders exhibited a mastery of color, form, and texture, incorporating sculptural evergreens and yuccas, broad-leaved bergenia, and acanthus. These provided the framework, which she filled in with flowers—a drift of one kind of hardy plant or wildflower flowing gracefully into the next. The picture that resulted appeared natural and effortless, even easy. She countered that nothing could be further from the truth. In her book *Colour Schemes for the Garden* (1908), she wrote: "Those who do not know are apt to think that hardy flower gardening of the best kind is easy. It is not easy at all. It has taken me half a lifetime merely to find out what is best worth doing, and a good slice of another half to puzzle out ways of doing it."

Jekyll wrote a series of articles for *The Garden Club of America Bulletin.* In the March 1920 issue, she advocated using the term "flower border," calling it "the simplest name for the border that is to hold and display the best of our hardy flowers with any admixture of tender plants that may be desirable. Quite commonly it is called the herbaceous border, but many of its indispensable occupants are not herbaceous; or it is called the hardy flower border, but that name, too, loses its justification when we fill up with tender plants and half-hardy annuals. Therefore it had better be simply—the Flower Border. . . . Moreover, it is certainly more important that the border shall be beautiful than that it should be either strictly hardy or herbaceous."

On the following pages we will visit beautiful flower borders, to use Jekyll's preferred term, often backed by stonewalls, then beds of flowers brightening an expanse of lawn. Beds and borders devoted to roses will follow, with several pictures showing the drama of shrub roses planted en masse. And finally we shall come to some cutting gardens that would set any flower arranger's heart aflutter.

All of this is happening in American gardens where, even without the benevolent English climate, gardeners are painting with flowers.

BORDERS

previous page ❀ Peonies and dahlias join the delphiniums in Martha Hamilton Morris's garden in Villanova, Pennsylvania. The wall behind the border wraps around the garden giving the house, which is named Cotswold, a very Cotswold feeling. Shortly before this photograph was taken, the garden was the scene of a double wedding reception for two Morris daughters.

right ❀ The stone wall backdrop, the topiaries, and clipped hedge all lend importance to this perennial border in Colleen Hempleman's garden in Greenwich, Connecticut, but it is the delphiniums that steal the show. Daylilies provide the second act in midsummer.

overleaf, left ❀ A bountiful border and tranquil terrace introduce visitors to the charm of Joan Duddingston's garden in St. Paul, Minnesota. Many of the border's plants were started from seed under Gro-Lights when Joan could not find the cultivars she wanted in nurseries. Joan considers zone hardiness labels simply a challenge. Last year ten cotton plants flowered and produced cotton balls in her Minnesota garden. This year's focus is a hardy banana tree.

overleaf, right ❀ Shrub roses play a starring and supporting role in Marge Hols's St. Paul, Minnesota, perennial border. The house is a 1909 Tudor villa home on a historic avenue that stretches four miles from the state capitol to the Mississippi River. The street is considered the "best-preserved example of a Victorian monumental residential boulevard in the United States." The Hols property adds to the mystique, with an English cottage-style garden visible through the wrought-iron fence.

opposite *My garden is not low-maintenance, but I don't care. I love working in it and spend as much time there as possible.*

The garden holds so many attractions for me—the challenge of just keeping plants alive in this harsh climate, the challenge of composing beautiful combinations, satisfaction for my need to keep learning, the fun of propagating lots of plants, a quiet refuge where I can lose myself in the task at hand. The joy, as they say, is in the journey.

MARGE HOLS, ST. PAUL, MINNESOTA

left ❖ If you're planning a bed instead of a border, garden designers suggest you make two of them. Penelope Harris's garden in Wyndmoor, Pennsylvania, illustrates the value of that advice. Smooth stone separates the beds from the lawn and frames the diptych of colors, textures, and forms that echo back and forth. To Penelope, these two beds "look like Persian carpet runners." She says, "This garden evolved from three beds to four beds, to complete exhaustion. Rethinking and redesign brought it to its present two beds, simplified and now manageable."

overleaf, left ❖ The same structural engineer who installed Gwen Babcock's walkway (page 52) created these terraced beds along the descent. Gwen has filled them with agave, aloe, Zwartkop aeonium (in bloom in the distance), and other drought-tolerant succulents mixed with nasturtiums. Her San Marino, California, garden benefits from warm air rising up the hill, making it five degrees warmer than it is a block away. After the path makes a turn, the scene changes to daylilies, nicotiana, mahonia, geranium, and statice, with amaryllis that Gwen puts in the ground after they've finished their Christmastime show.

overleaf, right ❖ Borders and beds in shades of pink and lavender with rings of white fill one of many rooms in this Illinois garden. The central beds are anchored on the four corners by mounds of boxwood and centered by urns.

opposite *One October we visited cousins in Vermont. They were cutting everything down, "putting the garden to bed." To bed? How wonderful. There's no rest for the California gardener. We garden 365 days a year. Of course, we have orange juice every day of the year too. And if I deadhead every single day, many of my plants will bloom 365 days a year.*

GWEN BABCOCK, SAN MARINO, CALIFORNIA

SIMPLY ROSES

right ✣ A circle of pale pink Bonica roses at the top of the drive gives a preview of what's to come in Pam Jeanes's flower-filled garden in Far Hills, New Jersey. An urn, surrounded by lavender and boxwood, has replaced a tree that once stood there.

overleaf ✣ An eight-foot lattice fence, fashioned after the one at Old Westbury Gardens on Long Island, protects Cissy Bryson's formal rose garden from deer and other critters in the Milwaukee, Wisconsin, suburb of Fox Point. The figure in the fountain is Edward Berge's *Wildflower* (c. 1920). In winter, the Bryson grandchildren dress her in a fur-trimmed red velvet doll's coat and hat. With snow at her feet and on the lattice tracery, it's a picture to rival the roses' display. Photo © Tony Casper.

When we moved into this neighborhood fifty years ago, we were the youngest on the block. Now we're the oldest. Our garden has evolved from a garden with two growing boys to a grown-up garden with two small dogs.

JOAN BANNING, PASADENA, CALIFORNIA

left ❖ Climbing roses, shrub roses, tree roses, and tea roses—in shades of pink, blush, white and palest yellow—fill Mary and Steven Read's cottage garden in Napa, California. In the background, near the front of the main house, are two standard white Iceberg roses, the first ones to be planted at Read's Leap. The variety and color have been carried throughout the property, unifying the areas.

above ❖ Passersby on this tree-lined Pasadena, California, street are treated to Cocktail, a modern shrub rose, at eye level and, at foot level, a border of aeonium tumbling over a low wall constructed from recycled sidewalk pieces. Inside the fence is a cottage garden that has been lovingly tended by Joan Banning for fifty years.

 *above* *I have made endless forays to nurseries from Long Island's swish Hamptons to Maine's craggy coast. I should have had a bumper sticker that said "I brake for nurseries." I would arrive home by moonlight to unload my caravan before crawling joyfully into bed, my little head dancing with knowing that I had captured the loveliest plants imaginable. These plants I knew would make the perfect combinations, produce the most exquisite bouquets. My heart would leap and my pocketbook would wane.*

PAULINE RUNKLE, THE GARDEN AT THREE PLUM HILL, MANCHESTER-BY-THE-SEA, MASSACHUSETTS

opposite *Two days before the garden was to be on the Garden Conservancy's Open Days, I awoke to a crying daughter and gardener! The deer, for the first time ever, had invaded my garden and eaten all of the Chianti roses. There must have been 250; the garden was loaded. Then they came brazenly in and helped themselves to at least half of the other roses! I called the police! (I didn't know what else to do!) They sent a young man to my house from sundown to sunup for the next two nights. He went around the garden every hour with a powerful flashing light and a tambourine-type noisemaker. The deer did not return that year or the next.*

JANE FOSTER, MOUNT DESERT ISLAND, MAINE

✻ If ever a garden was planted to be a cutting garden, it is this one in Manchester-by-the-Sea, Massachusetts. Early in Pauline Runkle's career as a floral artist, she longed for garden flowers to punctuate her signature mass arrangements. When she found this four-acre property in 1984, it was a deserted pig farm—the house had burned—with dead trees and rusted mattress springs dotting the landscape. She looked beyond those to the granite outcroppings and movement of the land and to what might be and now is.

above ✻ Jane Foster's cutting garden runs into the woods behind her Mount Desert Island, Maine, house. This and perennial borders in front allow Jane to fill her house with flowers.

above ❈ Inside an eight-foot-high yew hedge
in Bunny and Juan O'Callahan's Stonington,
Connecticut, garden are eleven beds dedicated
to bulbs, roses, perennials, bushes, berries, and
vegetables. The cutting garden sections offer
daffodils and then tulips in the spring, followed
by Siberian iris, oriental poppies, and peonies.
Summer, pictured here, brings bearded iris, phlox,
coreopsis, and false indigo, to name a few.

opposite ❈ Early Colonial designs inspired raised
geometric beds and the contents of this Milwaukee
herb and cutting garden. The central beds hold
fragrant, culinary, and medicinal plants while
perennials flower on both sides of a picket fence
fashioned after a seventeenth-century template.
The property, home to Anne and Fred Vogel and
known as Pickerel Run, sits on the ancient site
of a Native American camp where Indian Creek,
formerly called Pickerel Run, flows into the
Milwaukee River.

opposite We put up an electric fence to keep the deer out of the cutting garden, because they devoured the roses and trampled the vegetables. After about five years, the electric part of the fence gave out, so we just had the wires up—which seemed to work just fine. This year we've taken the wires down and hope the memory of a shocked nose is still with the family of deer.

BUNNY O'CALLAHAN, SALT ACRES, STONINGTON, CONNECTICUT

above Our nation's origins are deeply rooted in seventeenth-century New England, and it is the decorative arts and architecture from this early period that have interested and inspired us as owners of this woodland property in Milwaukee. The herb garden, transformed from our family campground, provides grand and magical vistas of the Milwaukee River, revealing the four seasons in all their glory along this natural corridor. It is amazing to think that native woodland hunter-gatherers set up fishing circles in the river and work stations on the very shore where we garden today.

ANNE VOGEL, PICKEREL RUN, MILWAUKEE, WISCONSIN

7 The Magic of Color

FASHIONS IN GARDEN COLOR COME AND GO, BUT AT PRESENT THE OPTIONS ARE MORE varied than ever. Perhaps we owe this, in part, to Fletcher Steele, who designed the famous Blue Steps at Naumkeag. In his book *Gardens and People* (1964), he attacked those with strong prejudices against certain colors:

> Some people seem to think that refinement consists of a collection of prejudices—they will not have this, and they cannot bear that. Vulgar is their favorite epithet. They cringe at anything vivid. Their colors must be "soft" and they talk of "pastel shades."

> Once it got red out of sight, prejudice made a nuisance of other colors. Magenta was sent to the doghouse and bright yellow put on probation. In time even admittedly agreeable tones were stripped away by faddists till in the most expensive borders only blue flowers or white were allowed.

> When this purge of color got well under way, all plants were outlawed whose foliage was not entirely green, on the pretext that they were 'unnatural.' (As though Nature could be ashamed by rules of etiquette!)

> The unbiased artist knows that all colors and all foliage have a place somewhere in his work, like words in the dictionary waiting for a poet.

> All colors are beautiful or ugly according to their quantity and place in relation to other colors. Any arbitrary elimination removes a possible source of pleasure.

> Why put your eye on a diet?

Color is probably the one element that writes the garden owner's signature on the landscape. A fondness for pastels is evident in every picture of Mary Read's Napa garden. Pamela Smith's garden in Carmel-by-the-Sea, California, glows with yellows, oranges, and reds. But even a garden that is characterized by one color combination can change pace in a bed or corner. In her garden on Mount Desert Island, Maine, Jane Foster focuses on pinks and purples and blues in her perennial border. But there are yellow dahlias and deep salmon zinnias in her cutting garden. Nearby, the cardinal flower (*Lobelia cardinalis*) is planted with the reds and burgundies of coleus and other hot foliage in what Jane calls her "hotbed of discontent."

Color, as Jekyll and other designers are quick to point out, is not limited to flowers. Evergreens come in endless shades of green, gray-green, green-blue, golden green. The burgundy foliage of cannas and the great variety to be found in coleuses have made these once looked-down-upon plants popular again. Succulents offer an artist's palette of colors along with sculptural forms. As we continue our garden walk, we'll see how garden designers and gardeners have painted with plants, some in pastels, some in "knock-your-socks-off" colors. The subtler shades demand a second, thoughtful look. The bright and bold excite and delight.

I was pleased to host many visiting garden tours over the years, not only from the United States but also from New Zealand, France, and the UK. Visitors often expressed surprise and delight when viewing the garden from the upper terrace—allowing them to appreciate its design. That was a great compliment to the modern architecture of the home as well as to the design of the garden.

CAROL VALENTINE, SANTA BARBARA, CALIFORNIA

previous pages ✣ Tree ferns (*Dicksonia antarctica*) create a green bower in Helen Hickingbotham's garden in Hillsborough, California. A white birdbath provides contrast to the green and brings the scene to life. Thomas Church returned to the Hickingbotham garden three times, adding rooms and features, including a path that leads from the visitors' parking area into this oasis.

opposite and overleaf ✣ Areas of a single, subtle color cause the viewer to focus on form and texture in Carol Valentine's garden.

above ✣ Noted landscape designer Isabelle Greene designed this revolutionary bit of landscaping in the 1980s for and with her friend Carol Valentine. Santa Barbara was in the midst of a six-year drought, with very low water allocations; the steep slope was a second challenge. Their joint solution was an abstract garden with water suggested by flows and pools of slate; lushness and color were achieved with drought-tolerant plants such as agave, yucca, evergreen candytuft, and snow-in-summer. From the balcony, the terracing of the slope is evident, with softly colored concrete forming beds filled with sculptural plants and masses of succulents in cool and warm colors. The abstract pattern recalls an aerial view of farming fields and terraced hillsides of rice paddies, the soft glint of slate suggesting the movement of water. This is indeed art painted with plants.

When we lived downtown, the neighborhood was clean and green—grass and junipers. People were always out there clipping and mowing. We put in a rock garden of alpines at the front of the house. Neighbors saw how low-maintenance it was and said, "We're going to do a xeriscape like yours!"

PANAYOTI KELAIDIS, DENVER, COLORADO

above and opposite ❀ Panayoti Kelaidis likes the pink of Pike's Peak granite as a foil for the green and gray of rock-garden plants. To create a new rock-garden area near his house, Kelaidis, director of outreach and designer of the alpine garden at the Denver Botanic Garden, moved in sixty tons of the pink stone. When it came time to redo the kitchen, he chose Pike's Peak granite for the countertops, the only instance he knows of in which the kitchen was designed to match the garden.

Kelaidis has 5,000 plants in his present garden, where he's been for twelve years, and 2,000 in his first garden, where he was for nine years. Two-thirds of his plants are from seed or from trading with other rock-garden enthusiasts. If he buys a new variety, he will buy three plants—one to plant at his current residence in sandy soil, one in clay that retains moisture at his former downtown residence, and one at the Denver Botanic Garden. Often only one will thrive.

above ✢ The dark, rough-textured stones in Susan Deeks's rock garden in New Vernon, New Jersey, were salvaged from a defunct arsenal. Now they hold dwarf evergreens and alpines that Susan grows from seeds. "New Jersey is not the ideal place for alpines," she says, "but the sheer perversity of the location and climate makes me humble and makes me relish any and all successes."

opposite ✢ Tall zebra mallows (*Malva sylvestris* 'Zebrina') and spiderwort (*Tradescantia*) are complemented by the subtle color and interesting texture of Martha Hamilton Morris's Villanova, Pennsylvania, home.

When I was younger, I lived on this lane right next door to Mrs. Dulles, the charming, wonderful, kind lady who built the house we now live in, and I was devoted to her. She moved into the house when she was thirty-one, had three daughters, and lived here fifty-eight years.

Upon Mrs. Dulles's death, we were told by her family that she had hoped that if no one in her family wanted to live in the house, we would do so. We moved here thirty-three years ago. I was thirty-one, have three daughters, and hope to be here at least twenty-five more years!

MARTHA HAMILTON MORRIS, VILLANOVA, PENNSYLVANIA

BOLD AND BRIGHT

above ✿ Dahlias flourish in Jenny Lynn Bradley's garden in Highlands, North Carolina, where the 4,000-foot elevation means cool days and nights. No shrinking violets here. Jenny Lynn explains her selection: "They are in knock-your-socks-off, in-your-face colors, garish and bold, and I cannot wait to see them bloom each summer."

right ✿ A color triad has its own magic, here created with green box, blue pansies, and Apricot Beauty tulips. New Zealand flax, in the urn, introduces a contrast of textures in Virginia Spencer's garden in Birmingham, Alabama.

left ✤ People drive for miles to see the state flower blooming in the Antelope Valley California Poppy Reserve, a state park—or they swing by Pamela Smith's driveway in Carmel-by-the-Sea, where self-seeding *Eschscholzia californica*, which blooms for six months, is mixed with just enough deep blue and green for contrast.

above ✤ The hot colors of two natives, cardinal flower (*Lobelia cardinalis*) and black-eyed Susan (*Rudbeckia hirta*), are welcome in the cool mountains of Highlands, North Carolina, where Jenny Lynn Bradley has her summer garden.

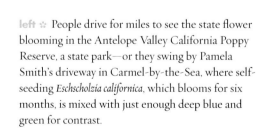

opposite ✣ Just inside the gate of Pamela Smith's garden is another scene alive with color, but these pincushion protea (*Leucospermum cordifolium* 'Tango') are native to South Africa, not California. They bloom for four or five months.

above ✣ The vibrant reds and yellows in the Olympic Flame tulips are repeated in solid-colored tulips beyond the sculpture in Louisa Duemling's garden in the Georgetown section of Washington, D.C. A white azalea cools the scene.

overleaf, left, top ✣ Three blue spheres—open metal balls—are used as accents in this Chester, New Jersey, garden. Jeanne Will says, "They live in various places as the mood moves us. The juxtaposition of manmade objects and living plants seems to prompt the brain to focus more fully on all the elements in the scene."

overleaf, left, bottom ✣ Butterfly and beetle pause on ceramic leaves that Carolyn Kroh made and fired in her kiln. More surround the small pond in her Shawnee Mission, Kansas, garden, where water lettuce and other aquatics flourish in summer. Next pottery project: ceramic mushrooms for the garden.

overleaf, right ✣ A Japanese umbrella in saffron yellow calls visitors' attention to the prickly leafed gunnera it is shading at Iron Mountain Farm in Portland, Oregon.

top *I find it fascinating how much you can learn about people and cultures from observing and studying their gardens.*

JEANNE WILL, HEDGEROWS, CHESTER, NEW JERSEY

bottom *Tornadoes and the Wizard of Oz are never far away. It is said that the West begins in Kansas City, and this is certainly true of our western drying winds.*

CAROLYN KROH, SHAWNEE MISSION, KANSAS

above ❖ A vermillion Chinese-style gazebo was the stamp Alice Houston and her husband James put on the garden of the historic Captain Amos Palmer House in Stonington, Connecticut, when they moved there in 1983. The house has a colorful history, beginning with Captain Palmer, a privateer, who built it with his share of bounty in 1787. The artist James McNeill Whistler lived here as a child, and Stephen Vincent Benét had his writing room on the top floor. James Houston is recognized for having brought Inuit art, such as the bone, stone, and ceramic sculpture pictured here, to world attention.

opposite ❖ The red of two Adirondack chairs make the lush lawn in Jill Josselyn Scheer's Portland, Oregon, garden look even greener.

8 Nature Trained and Contained

FROM THE EARLIEST MOMENTS OF "THE GARDEN"—PERHAPS THE EGYPTIAN GARDENS revealed on tomb paintings—people have moved, bent, clipped, and shaped nature's plant material to their vision. There have been periods when a return to nature urged the would-be garden designer to leave well enough alone, but the art and love of shaping plant material has survived every turn of fashion. In this section, we will look at a number of ways in which gardeners and garden designers train and contain nature's plant material.

First there is the shaping of plant material into geometric forms—spheres of clipped box or yew in the garden, cubes of foliage atop trees. These strong forms send a strong message: This is a formal, dignified space with Italian and French influences.

The second style to be explored is the parterre, planting in a pattern. This, too, carries the message of formality and calls to mind the grand designs at Versailles and the knot gardens of England. It also speaks of skill in the planning and planting, and of commitment in the maintenance.

Planting in a pattern on a larger scale could describe the maze on page 154. The terms "maze" and "labyrinth" are often used interchangeably, even in the dictionary, but enthusiasts of both forms make a distinction. Maze more often represents a puzzle, a pattern with options and dead ends, in which finding your way to the center and out again is a challenge. Labyrinth, on the other hand, is a path that leads without deviation to the center and back again.

Topiary, the pruning and training of trees and shrubs into fanciful forms, is referred to in Pliny the Elder's *Naturalis Historia,* published in A.D.77. Pliny describes cypress trees that have been cut and trained to represent hunting scenes, ships in sail, and indeed "all sorts of images." More than a thousand years later, in Renaissance Florence, the art was reborn. Accounts of the Rucellai garden, started in 1459, mention "spheres, porticoes, temples, vases, urns, apes, donkeys, oxen, a bear, giants, men, women."

Penelope Hobhouse notes in *The Story of Gardening* (2002) that the use of topiary reached its apogee in the gardens of seventeenth- and eighteenth-century France and spread from there to England and throughout Europe. Although much of England's topiary fell victim to Capability Brown's landscape movement in England, it nevertheless lived on in grand gardens in Europe and in cottage gardens.

Bonsai, one of the most ancient of arts, was first practiced in China, the earliest record discovered on a tomb from 706. Buddhist monks brought the art to Japan during the Heian Period (A.D.794–1191), when it became a pursuit limited to royalty. The earliest representation of it in Japan appears on a scroll dated 1195. The art of bonsai, or "tray-planting" as it translates, continues to fascinate—that so much of life and time can be contained, constrained in such small and exquisite forms.

The final pictures of this section show how a hardscape—either vertical, such as a wall, or horizontal, such as a paved court or terrace—can be softened by carefully trained and contained plant material. There are artists at work here—with clippers.

previous page ❖ Trees in formal shapes are featured in the enclosed garden, named "Cocoon," of Lucy Reno's townhome in Carmel Valley, California. A restricted palette of green and white adds to the formality and serenity.

above ❖ Balls of Burford holly, planted perhaps eighty years ago by the former owners, Mr. and Mrs. J. V. G. Posey, line the central axis of Anne and James Crumpacker's garden in Portland, Oregon, leading the eye to a reflecting pool at the end of the lawn. Mrs. Posey, a knowledgeable and dedicated gardener, was president of the Portland Garden Club. It was said that she would rather have a load of manure than a new dress.

right ❖ Groups of trees in formal shapes are one way in which British landscape architect Martin Lane Fox related the landscaping of Carolands, Ann Johnson's home in Hillsborough, California, to the chateau's seventeenth-century style.

Seven years ago, we left our house and beloved garden of thirty-five years to move to a retirement community. My husband of fifty-seven years said it was time, and I agreed—if I could have a garden.

Our previous garden was on many garden tours, including the Pennsylvania Horticultural Society's, but I didn't expect any tours here. However, the Shipley School Secret Gardens Tour was here last week and the Gladwyne Library Tour will be here on Tuesday. We were amazed at the number of people who came and expressed a great interest in our small garden. The rest of the gardens were large and impressive, but so many of us are getting older!

LANA CRAWFORD, GLADWYNE, PENNSYLVANIA

above ✿ Lana and Russell Crawford of Gladwyne, Pennsylvania, asked friend and nurseryman Chuck Gale to design their retirement villa "garden." His answer to the postage-stamp-size space was a parterre, now filled with cherry laurel encircled by Japanese holly and edged with juniper. It's a cool green scene all year, brightened by a border of Delaware Valley White azaleas in the spring.

opposite ✿ "Architectural, simple, evergreen, having a sense of order and purpose, creating a mood of peace and calm," is how Ruthie Bowlin describes her Memphis, Tennessee, garden. "I choose plants for their form and texture, once planting a hundred Annabel hydrangeas in an area for the effect of a solid plane of green." She adds, "Evening parties are a priority. Forms and patterns become more dramatic at twilight."

opposite *I love the garden because I can make it mine and not have to listen to anyone else. I try to listen to the land and hear what it has to say.*

LOUISE WRINKLE, BIRMINGHAM, ALABAMA

opposite ✿ The boxwood parterre was planted in the 1950s by Louise Wrinkle's mother, but the openwork espalier of native crabapple (*Malus angustifolia*) was her idea. "Experts" suggested a wall, a fence, or a hedge to block off the parking court from this sunken garden. Instead, Wrinkle planted individual trees in an X pattern, with a bigger tree anchoring each end. Crabapple blossoms and tulips—White Triumphator and black Queen of Night—herald spring in this part of the Birmingham, Alabama, garden.

above ✿ An armillary sphere with signs of the zodiac repeats the curves of the parterre filled with roses in Colleen Hempleman's Greenwich, Connecticut, garden.

above ❖ The fine texture of the parterre is in dramatic contrast to the foliage of the white bird-of-paradise (*Strelitzia nicolai*) in the background in Kit Pannill's Palm Beach, Florida, garden.

opposite ❖ A knot garden of boxwood (*Buxus* 'Green Velvet') is patterned after an inlay on an early eighteenth-century Pennsylvania chest. As they developed their garden on the banks of the Milwaukee River, Anne and Fred Vogel looked to the early colonists for design inspiration, just as the colonists had looked to England. Ann Leighton's 1970 book, *Early American Gardens for Meate or Medicine,* and correspondence with the author were especially helpful.

above ✣ Visitors can explore a seven-foot-tall circular maze in Elizabeth and William Martin's garden in Essexville, Michigan. Created from 300 yews (*Taxus* x *media* 'Hicksii') planted in 1989, the design is based on a pattern from the British Museum.

right ✣ A couple of inches' difference—between very short and slightly longer grass—makes possible this turf labyrinth in an Illinois garden. Tradition has it that whatever issue comes to mind as you enter the pattern is dwelt on as you walk the circles. By the time you emerge, the conflict is resolved, the problem solved. A famous labyrinth in the floor of Chartres Cathedral in France was built about A.D. 1200.

opposite ✣ If maze explorers persevere, they will be rewarded with the barely audible sound of water as it bubbles into a pool. They can rest on curved benches and enjoy the alpine plants tucked among the rocks before beginning their journey out of the maze in the Martins' Michigan garden.

left ❀ Fifty-year-old ivy seahorse topiaries "swim" in an underwater fantasy of twisted wisteria vines and floating blossoms, all in Berenice Spalding's Hillsborough, California, garden. Watching over the scene is one of two known statues of *St. Francis of Assisi* by American sculptor Frances Rich.

overleaf, left ❀ The menagerie at Topiary Fancies, Lucy Day's Greenwich, Connecticut, garden, is designed to amuse and amaze visitors. Inspired by Green Animals in Portsmouth, Rhode Island; Ladew Topiary Garden in Monkton, Maryland; travels in England; and the need to start from scratch after major construction, the Days decided on a bold new vision. Lucy said, "Our intention was to design and commission large topiaries sited so each turn in the garden provides a surprise and each view from the house frames a vignette." Here we see what is known as the Llama Garden.

overleaf, right ❀ Lucy Day introduces us to William and Henry, sitting Sphinxlike in front of an equally regal terrace in her Greenwich, Connecticut, garden. Steve Manning, the designer, came from England and lived with the Days for three weeks while he shaped the aluminum frames and installed the internal watering system. The bodies are covered in sod, which needs trimming about once a week in growing season. The manes and tufts on the tails are of grasslike sweet flag (*Acorus gramineus* 'Variegatus'). The "boys" look particularly nice with a dusting of snow.

My love of gardening came relatively late in life. I retired from a career on Wall Street when I turned forty and became a full-time volunteer. Suddenly I had time to learn about gardens and to appreciate them. I took classes at the New York Botanical Garden and at the Garden Education Center of Greenwich. I love visiting gardens, growing and showing and learning. I love our topiary garden's humor, its sense of surprise—textures and beauty in all seasons. I love the effect it has on visitors. It is great for entertaining. I love seeing it out of every window, walking around it, sitting in it.

LUCY DAY, GREENWICH, CONNECTICUT

159

above ✼ After planting what she refers to as "three deer delicatessens," Carol Sullivan walled in her Pebble Beach, California, garden. The wall makes a fine backdrop for the meticulously pruned box and her collection of thirty bonsai ranging in age from five to seventy-five years old.

right ✼ Many of the 200 bonsai in Bonny and David Martin's Memphis, Tennessee, garden reside on benches, while others add their exotic touch to terraces and pools in the Japanese-style landscape. A devotee of bonsai since 1965 and founder of the Memphis Bonsai Society, Bonny makes it clear that bonsai is not low-maintenance gardening. The dwarfed trees in shallow containers require daily watering, year round, even three times a day in hot, dry summers. New growth requires frequent pinching, and, although they are trees, the bonsai are moved to a cool greenhouse for the Tennessee winters, when temperatures can drop to zero, heaving up roots and breaking containers.

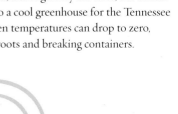

above ❖ A brick retaining wall in Louise Wrinkle's Birmingham, Alabama, garden is embossed with the pattern and texture of Confederate jasmine (*Trachelospermum jasminoides*) coaxed into diamond shapes. It was originally trained on a framework of weedeater line stretched between nails in the brick wall. The nails held the vine slightly away from the wall, so the new growth could be wrapped around the line. The jasmine has been winter-killed only once in its twenty years; it grew back from the roots.

opposite ❖ Some garden artists "draw" with plant material, and Bettie Beardon Pardee is one of them. A wall space between two windows of her Newport, Rhode Island, home becomes a canvas on which to train a pyracantha in ascending circles. The composition changes color according to the season.

overleaf ❖ Landscape designer Deborah Nivens transformed the flat expanse of a Houston, Texas, courtyard into contemporary art with clipped mounds of yaupon holly (*Ilex vomitoria* and *I. vomitoria* 'Bordeaux'). Yaupon holly is native to Texas and is described as "growing anywhere—in full sun or shade, seaside or swamp, sand or clay." Other native plants and pots of citrus provide contrast in what is called the Texas Garden.

9 A World of Containers

IT HAS BEEN SAID THAT ANYTHING YOU CAN GROW IN THE GROUND YOU CAN GROW in a pot. And, perhaps more to the point, many things you cannot grow in the ground can be grown in pots. Adverse conditions—a lack of space; simply not enough ground in which to plant; the wrong space with too much shade or too much sun; soil that is too heavy or too porous; too little or too much water for the plant you want to grow—all can be corrected if the plant is put in a pot. Desert plants can be planted in a friendly medium and protected from excessive rainfall. Bog plants can be given their extra requirement of moisture. Delicate blossoms can be protected from the noonday sun with colorful umbrellas placed near the pots, as the Japanese do.

The advantages of plants in pots do not end with the right amount of light, soil, and water supply. Those factors are just the beginning. The true appeal is the design role that pots can play in your garden—from the cheerful pot of annuals at the back door to the elegant urn that draws the eye and the visitor to the outermost reaches of your property.

George Drower in *Garden of Invention* (2003) traces the history of plants in containers to Rameses III, born in 1198 B.C., who established hundreds of semipublic gardens and embellished them with flowerpots. The use of pots continued down through history. City-dwelling Romans used potted plants on rooftops to bring a bit of the countryside into the crowded streets of the city. Paintings of Renaissance gardens in Italy show pots marking the corners of parterres and arranged along the tops of walls. The gardens of Louis XIV of France introduced the square planters on legs called Versailles boxes that are still popular today.

With the popularity of glasshouses in the nineteenth century, pots were essential both for holding large specimens and for growing the thousands (millions?) of tender plants used in bedding-out schemes.

Trough gardening, currently a popular version of container gardening, has its own history. The troughs were originally stone watering or feed troughs for farm animals. In the 1920s and 1930s, as metal and lighter materials became available, the cumbersome stone troughs were set aside, and English gardeners soon took them up—probably as part of the rage for rock gardening that Reginald Farrer had started a decade earlier. His 1907 book *My Rock Garden* was so popular that by 1930 it was in its eighth printing. Troughs, English gardeners understood, could be drilled and layered with Farrer's "ideal rock-garden mixture," creating the perfect environment. Furthermore, the average cottage dweller could find a spot for them in the garden. A grand estate was not necessary.

Today's troughs are for the most part lightweight and are made in endless shapes and sizes. Many pictured here were created by the gardeners themselves. HGTV and the Internet offer "recipes" and instructions. The troughs and containers that follow illustrate clearly that container gardening is an art, not just a means. Panayoti Kelaidis says, "Consider the trough a frame. You are painting a picture inside it." Let's continue our visit in a world of containers, alone and grouped to create landscaping statements and drama by repetition.

✿ *A part of me has been in the garden since I was a very young child. My earliest memories include the harvesting of vegetables from my small patch in a communal garden on an old estate in Short Hills and savoring, for perhaps the tenth time, that favorite book* The Secret Garden, *which tells of the reawakening spirits of three young children as they explore a magical and mysterious walled garden. I knew early on that horticulture in its many manifestations could infuse our lives with newness and beauty and surprises and challenges and solace and spiritual growth. It was part hard labor and part library research and part sheer bliss. Above all, the wonderful fellow gardeners I met along the way ratified this choice.*

My husband, Dan, and I moved to a small farm in the rolling hills of western New Jersey. It had never had a garden, and even on a snowy January day the property seemed to be waiting for someone to bring it to life.

Over the past twenty years the garden has expanded and been shaped by our changing moods, by studying the effects of light and shade, and by what some might call the obsessive acquisition of new plants. We try to select species with interesting bark or colorful leaf patterns or with seasons of importance. The garden unfolds in a series of different themes as you walk through, and you never quite know what might lie ahead.

We have lots of critters who have gourmet appetites, but a dear friend and city dweller said to me years ago, "You have so much to share with the birds and rabbits and chipmunks," and I have thought of that ever since, and just planted a little more closely or pruned a little less tightly and for the most part we seem to have made peace.

JEANNE WILL, HEDGEROWS, CHESTER, NEW JERSEY

previous page ❧ Lois Baylis took a workshop on how to make troughs in 1992 and now she gives four or five workshops a year to others. Marc Keane, landscape architect and author of *Japanese Garden Design,* helped design this area of her Darien, Connecticut, garden to showcase troughs planted with alpines and conifers.

opposite ❧ Hedgerows, Jeanne Will's garden in Chester, New Jersey, is one of the most sought-after destinations for visiting-garden tours. Discriminating and knowledgeable members of the North American Rock Garden, the Tri-State Hosta, the Hardy Plant, and the Daphne Societies have all found much to delight them there. If, however, you ask Jeanne what her favorite is in this exceptional garden, she singles out her troughs. "I love our troughs," she explains. "These gardens in miniature offer so much to the quiet observer. I think in my dotage, I will be happy just surrounded by troughs. There is no limit to the variety of plants you can grow." A few of her troughs surround a pool on the terrace.

left ❧ Many of Susan Deeks's rock garden seedlings find homes in trough gardens assembled in a corner of her terrace in New Vernon, New Jersey.

overleaf, left ❧ Each of Carol Valentine's containers holds a composition, a painting with plants chosen for their color, form, and textural interest, then complemented with rocks, gravel, and pieces of colored pottery. They grace the terrace of her Santa Barbara, California, home.

overleaf, right ❧ A moss-covered frame filled with cactus-type potting soil serves as a container for this living wreath on Marge Hols's front gate in St. Paul, Minnesota. It winters over in a garage or sunroom.

left ❊ An arrangement of succulents in containers and other works of art on Carol Valentine's terrace glisten in the early morning Santa Barbara fog.

above ✿ Finding this large stone planter—
discarded and in pieces—was one of many surprises
that awaited Jill Josselyn Scheer and her husband
when they bought their 1922 home in Portland,
Oregon, fifteen years ago. Wired together, it now
holds white Iceberg roses underplanted with white
alyssum.

opposite ✿ A white camellia in a glazed, decorated
pot and a grouping of pink roses anchors one corner
of the pool terrace in Helen Hickingbotham's
garden in Hillsborough, California.

opposite ✤ These two vessels on Joan Donner's terrace hold a lot of history. Reproductions in Fiberglas by artist Bruce Haughy, the one on the left takes its design from an Anasazi piece made about A.D. 1100 in the Tularosa Basin of south central New Mexico. The design on the right dates from about A.D. 900 and the Ananzi Indians of eastern Arizona.

The vessels, native plantings, and adobe wall blend into the distant shrubland and Cheyenne Mountains. Joan Donner is not surprised to see bears, mountain lions, bobcats, foxes, or coyotes in her Colorado Springs garden. Deer frequently lie underneath a wind chime.

above ✤ Texture and a graceful shape add interest to this terra-cotta container atop a moss-covered wall in Martha Hamilton Morris's garden in Villanova, Pennsylvania. One of a pair that has been passed down in the family, the container dates from the early 1900s.

above ❖ The broad leaves of hosta are brought to eye level, offering a pause in the parade of textures in Bunny O'Callahan's Stonington, Connecticut, garden. The blue glaze on the containers repeats the blue of Long Island Sound.

opposite ❖ Landscaping with pots softens the pool area, blending it into the surrounding plantings in Cecile McCaull's Greenwich, Connecticut, garden.

overleaf ❖ Containers of brighter blossoms throughout the garden contrast with and emphasize the deep burgundy of Japanese maples in Marilyn Asplundh's Bryn Athyn, Pennsylvania, garden.

above ❋ Three Japanese maples in matching pots are framed by brick pillars in Bonny and David Martin's Memphis, Tennessee, garden. Their growth is limited by the size of the container and by pruning, as are the many bonsai in Bonny's collection.

opposite ❋ If one iron planter of red-violet lantana and silver licorice plant is good, then five will be wonderful. Drama by repetition is clearly illustrated in this Illinois garden. Chartreuse lady's mantle (*Achillea mollis*) weaves the units into a whole.

overleaf, left ❋ Espaliered trees pick up the repetition where glazed blue-and-white containers leave off in Anne Coke's Dallas, Texas, garden. Anne buys plain terra-cotta pots, paints them with a white majolica glaze, adds a design in her favorite blue, and fires them in her kiln.

overleaf, right ❋ Dozens of terracotta containers overflowing with yellow pansies dance along the terrace walls in Berenice Spalding's Hillsborough, California, garden.

10 Particular Pleasures— Large and Small

IN THE GRANDEST OF GARDENS AND IN VERY MODEST GARDENS, AMONGST THE MANY pleasures offered at every turn, there are plants that stand out, that give particular pleasure to the owner and the visitor. Often these particular pleasures are trees—sometimes individuals or groups that the current owner planted, nurtured, and shaped—that are now showing signs of their mature stature. Carol Valentine's two espaliered fig trees offer an exquisite sculptural example.

Often, though, the trees that give pleasure day after day were planted decades or even a century before the current owners took up residence. These trees are gifts, inherited from a kindred spirit, that now become the responsibility, the charge, of the current owners. Anne and James Crumpacker in Portland, Oregon, see themselves as stewards of the Italianate garden that was mature before they moved in almost thirty years ago. Among the treasures is a Japanese maple that was grown from a seed collected in the garden of the Japanese emperor in 1935.

Trees punctuate or tower over the garden, forming much of what landscape designers call its "bones"— what remains when the flowers and foliage of summer and fall are gone. Winter in her Birmingham garden, Louise Wrinkle says, is her favorite time of year. "The air is clear and clean; there are no leaves or colored flowers to distract you, and you can see the bones of the garden as well as the lichen on the trees."

At the opposite end of the continuum—in size and permanence—are the woodland wonders that emerge in spring, small and fleeting. Louise Wrinkle is in her garden when those appear as well. "The spring ephemeral wildflowers sing their song before the bare trees leaf out." In her garden, finding an Asian "cousin" for the native wildflowers is part of the pleasure. The variegated Solomon's seal (*Polygonatum odoratum* 'Variegatum') from Asia now grows alongside the native green one (*Polygonatum biflorum*).

Then there are the "particular pleasures" that fall into neither the tall category of trees and vines nor the small category of woodland wonders. These plants offer their own particular kind of pleasure, possibly in their form and color and texture or in their size.

These are the joys that make a New England gardener keep a gangly bare stalk of *Brugmansia* in the garage all winter in anticipation of the days in midsummer when it will be crowned with eight-inch-long white trumpets. It is the act of faith that leads a gardener to prop up, once more, a fifty-year-old tree wisteria whose trunk is hollowed out by rot on the off chance that it might send out its white panicles yet one more time—and it does.

Rare, indeed, is the gardener who does not treasure the unusual, the rare. It is the thrill of the new and exotic that has sent plant explorers into the wilds of every continent on the planet in pursuit of more treasures, and it is the same thrill that sends modern-day explorers, notably Dan Hinckley, into the remote regions he describes in his book *The Explorer's Garden* (1999). A plant of merit and exquisite interest that is not seen in every garden has an appeal few gardeners can or would deny. In this section we take a closer look at these singular sensations, as well as some particular pleasures that have stood the test of time.

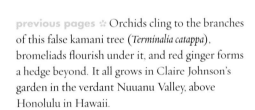

previous pages ✣ Orchids cling to the branches of this false kamani tree (*Terminalia catappa*), bromeliads flourish under it, and red ginger forms a hedge beyond. It all grows in Claire Johnson's garden in the verdant Nuuanu Valley, above Honolulu in Hawaii.

left ✣ Moss covers the branches of this Japanese maple (*Acer palmatum*) grown from seed collected in 1935 at the Shinjuku Imperial Garden in Tokyo by Mrs. Henry Cabell. Anne and James Crumpacker see themselves as stewards of this and many other treasures at Green Gate, their Portland, Oregon, garden.

above ✣ This multitrunked katsura (*Cercidiphyllum japonicum*) is more than a hundred feet tall and is thought to be more than a hundred years old. The largest in Connecticut and possibly in the world, it stands near Cecile and Phil McCaull's English manor-style house in Greenwich, and was a major selling point when they bought the property thirty years ago.

❀ *It is forty-five years of a growing and changing garden. It started with a few beds here and there, wherever I thought something would survive the children, dogs, cats, domestic rabbits, bantam game chickens, and domestic mallard ducks. The dogs made a path to the driveway gate, so that became a flagstone walk bordered by miniature shrubs, evergreen and shade-loving plants, with a few large stones from the Wissahickon Creek. The chickens loved to scratch out annuals, so we started to plant trees and shrubs. In those days, when we drove to the seashore we would buy a small birch for a dollar or two, and maybe a laurel.*

JOLY STEWART, FORGE FARM, AMBLER, PENNSYLVANIA

above ❊ Red horse chestnut blossoms (*Aesculus* x *carnea*) next to the warm tones of a Pennsylvania stone wall may be a happy coincidence on this farm in Ambler, Pennsylvania, but it's one that Joly Stewart plans to repeat, planting its "babies" along the pasture walls to mirror the winning combination.

opposite ❊ Adding its color to the spring scene of viburnum, Solomon's seal, and azaleas is a golden chain tree (*Laburnum* x *watereri*) in Jean Hudson's garden in Grosse Pointe Farms, Michigan. A stand of 200-year-old oaks, seen as visitors enter from the street, is also among the garden's pleasures.

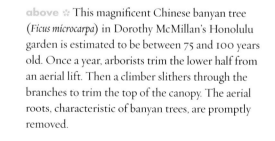

above ❖ This magnificent Chinese banyan tree (*Ficus microcarpa*) in Dorothy McMillan's Honolulu garden is estimated to be between 75 and 100 years old. Once a year, arborists trim the lower half from an aerial lift. Then a climber slithers through the branches to trim the top of the canopy. The aerial roots, characteristic of banyan trees, are promptly removed.

right ❖ The leaves of a variegated dogwood (*Cornus kousa* 'Gold Star') brighten a woodland scene in the Carson garden in Newtown Square, Pennsylvania.

overleaf ❖ A highlight of every spring, wisteria (*Wisteria sinensis*) emerges from a rock outcropping that matches it in strength and color in the Carsons' Newtown Square, Pennsylvania, garden.

above ❖ This native orchid, yellow lady's slipper (*Cypripedeum calceolus*), is a rare treat and sure to get a close look in Jeanne Will's woodland garden in Chester, New Jersey.

opposite ❖ Virginia sweetspire (*Itea virgínica* 'Henry's Garnet'), a native shrub, provides fragrant flowers and autumn color in Native Nook, Caroline Stevens's garden in Nashville, Tennessee.

overleaf ❖ Waves of daffodils flow toward Lake Toxaway at Lillian Balentine Law's summer home in Lake Toxaway, North Carolina. Photo © John Turner.

When my father and I would go on "missions" on Saturday morning—to check the rising sap in the sugar maples, to walk the fences for weak spots, or to fish for a plump bass, my father would quiz me: "What sign of spring is this pushing through the leaves?" I would proudly answer, "Dutchman's breeches." With a pat on my back, he often said, "We need to protect these friends of the forest." Fifty-plus years later, here at Native Nook, the theme of stewardship is being pursued and taught on less than an acre in an urban setting. Native Nook has set out to bring those plants overlooked or forgotten back into view by showcasing them as the backbone of our landscape structure.

As I seek to enhance the beauty of the neighborhood with native plants and to teach by example and through workshops, I feel that loving pat from childhood, accompanied by the phrase "We need to protect these friends of the forest."

CAROLINE STEVENS, NATIVE NOOK, NASHVILLE, TENNESSEE

above ❖ An antique hay rake recalls the Belgian farmers who originally settled the Grosse Pointe Farms area on Lake St. Clair in Michigan. In the late 1800s, summer homes were built along the lake, followed by grand estates at the turn of the century. Now wildflowers grow through the rake tines along Jean Hudson's woodland walk.

right ❖ A broad, mulched path leads visitors past native treasures, including *Phlox divaricata* and *Epimedium*, in this woodland garden in Washington, D.C. Only the mature trees were here when Louisa Duemling started the garden twelve years ago.

overleaf ❖ Pinkshell or vaseyi azaleas (*Rhododendron vaseyi*) are native to a very restricted region—four counties in North Carolina. Here they tumble down the mountainside below Lillian Balentine Law's summer home in Lake Toxaway, North Carolina. Photo © John Turner.

left ✿ Flowering kale (*Crambe maritima*) and giant allium (*Allium schubertii*) create an enchanting combination of grays and pinks in Gayle Maloney's perennial garden in Bernardsville, New Jersey. The dried allium heads, when painted red, blue, and silver, make great "sparklers" for children on the Fourth of July and, when painted black, "spiders" for Halloween.

right ✿ The pleasures in Carol Valentine's garden never end, as seen in this bit of exotica, a scallop echeveria (*Echeveria crenulata*), bejeweled with morning fog on her Santa Barbara terrace. The Southern California sun intensifies the coloring and "blistering" of the thickened leaves.

opposite ✿ Leland Miyano's garden in Kahalu'u, on Oahu, Hawaii, is filled with botanical wonders from around the world, including this enormous staghorn fern (*Platycerium superbum*). Eleven years before the photo was taken, it was a spore about the size of a quarter.

opposite *My garden began as a lawn when I bought it twenty-five years ago and is now a lowland rain forest, grown organically. It is an ecology-based garden depending primarily on natural rainfall, with a major component of Hawaiian native plants. At the moment the garden is somewhat an unruly adolescent. I have been taking out higher-maintenance items and planting more of the slow-growing Hawaiian natives. By slow—some of my seedlings took three years to germinate. Patience is key. I believe "Aloha" is an important word in the vocabulary of a good gardener. My favorite translation is: "In the presence of the breath of life."*

LELAND MIYANO, KAHALU'U, OAHU, HAWAII

above *I credit my mother for my love of gardening. She took me for walks to hunt for wildflowers in the western Massachusetts woods and fields. I planted my woodland garden in her memory, so I could grow the flowers I remember finding on our walks. The garden is completely secluded, and I love to sit there on the cedar bench and enjoy the spring show. It's my favorite spot in the garden.*

MARGE HOLS, ST. PAUL, MINNESOTA

opposite ✿ Subtle rather than showy is this clematis in Marge Hols's St. Paul, Minnesota, garden. Former Garden Club of America president Betty Corning discovered this clematis growing in a garden in Albany, New York, in 1933. The owner had been given a piece, stuck in a potato, by a friend—but had no idea of its name. A division of the plant, offered to Mrs. Corning, thrived. Researchers at the National Arboretum determined that it was an unnamed variety and suggested the name *Clematis* 'Betty Corning.' A Rochester clematis grower propagated it and made it available to botanic gardens, arboreta, and the public. The plant and Mrs. Corning received a number of prestigious awards during her lifetime.

above ✿ Very unusual indeed is this lush evergreen shrub in Pamela Smith's garden in Carmel-by-the-Sea, with its clusters of tubular blue flowers. *Lochroma cyanea* 'Indigo' is from Central and South America, and hummingbirds love it.

below ✿ The tulip-shaped blossoms of *Chiranthofremontia lenzii* 'Griff's Wonder' are the product of a hybridization between California flannel bush and the monkey-hand tree from Guatemala. Its colors are repeated in the South African pincushion protea (*Leucospermum cordifolium*) and complemented by chartreuse euphorbia in Pamela Smith's garden. "It's interesting to see how the colors and textures work together," Pam says. "I love the unusual."

11 The Garden as Gallery

RARE IS THE GARDEN THAT DOES NOT POSSESS SOME BIT OF SCULPTURAL ORNAMENTATION. At the smallest and simplest level, it might be a birdbath in the shape of a scallop shell, or a small statue of Saint Francis of Assisi, or a frog or cat figure tucked in amongst the hosta leaves. Often, the figures in larger gardens are casts of classical figures—Diana, Venus, the Four Seasons.

Although sculpture has been featured in gardens since the earliest times, it is Renaissance Italy that comes to mind most readily when sculpture and gardens are associated. When, in the fourteenth century, classical sculptures were excavated from the ruins of Greece and Rome, the Vatican took possession of the most important ones and placed them in the Belvedere Garden. Princely families such as the Medici acquired the next tier for their own gardens. Some of those treasured acquisitions can be seen today in the Boboli Gardens in Florence and in other Medici gardens.

The Italianate style of garden spread to Europe and reached its zenith in Le Nôtre's gardens at Versailles. When the original Greek or Roman statues were not available, casts were made and Versailles, though much altered, still has what is considered the finest collection of garden ornaments in the world.

The classical, orderly design of the Renaissance garden was the ideal setting for the ancient statuary, placed as it was in the center of a parterre or at the end of an axis or the meeting point of two *allées*. Classical figures still have their appeal and find their place in contemporary gardens, often in those that exhibit French and Italian influences.

But what about more contemporary art? Is there a place for that? Does it complement or conflict with the art that is the garden? Thomas Church, in *Gardens Are for People* (1955, 1983), has a definite opinion:

> After greenery, nothing, I believe, enhances a garden more than sculpture. Unlike flowers, it survives the changing seasons yet is not unchanging, for most sculpted materials not only weather but alter their appearance dramatically in different lights.

> Sculpture, statuary, wall plaques, and ceramics are not used enough in gardens, either through a fear of seeming pretentious or a lack of realization of what art can mean in the general composition.

> The old concept that statuary should dominate the area or should be at the end of every main axis and cross axis doesn't apply any more. It can be used casually on a wall or to brighten a corner of the garden.

On the following pages we will see how the garden is used as a museum, as a gallery space for the art that the garden owner loves—classical sometimes, often showcasing the beauty of the human figure. Then there are animals, wonderful realistic and whimsical animals, loose in the garden. And, finally, there is modern, abstract, even cutting-edge art. The placing of each piece in its garden setting is a creative act in its own right, comparable to the laying out of paths or the placing of a tree.

Let us tour these outdoor museums, giving time and thought to the art and its setting.

previous page ❀ A classical statue is classically sited in Elizabeth and William Martin's garden in Essexville, Michigan. An *allée* of European lindens (*Tilia cordata* 'Greenspire') frames an eighteenth-century lead figure, *The Shepherdess*. A double parterre of boxwood (*Buxus* 'Green Mountain') planted with watermelon-pink azaleas (*Rhododendron* 'Boudoir') surrounds the pedestal.

above ❀ A fountain with Allan Harris's sculpture *Diana* is backed by pink climbing roses and *Clematis* 'Etoile Violette.' Hybrid roses and heliotrope fill the surrounding bed, and herbs are featured in the central knot in Joly Stewart's Ambler, Pennsylvania, garden.

opposite ❀ Diana, goddess of the hunt, wears a cape of *Clematis* 'Rouge Cardinal' and C. 'Comtesse de Bouchaud' over one shoulder in this Illinois garden.

overleaf, left ❀ This bronze lady has been to sea many times, in the first-class lounge of HMS *Caronia*. When the Cunard luxury liner was decommissioned and sold for salvage, Pam Jeanes rescued a pair of these statues and placed them in her garden in Far Hills, New Jersey. They are underplanted with spirea to suggest rushing water.

overleaf, right ❀ Three Scottish children looking over a balcony are rendered in great detail in this nineteenth-century marble grouping. Elizabeth Martin has attached a wicker basket that she fills with lilies of the valley and other seasonal offerings from her Essexville, Michigan, garden.

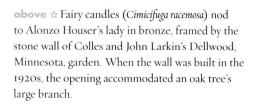 **above** ✿ Fairy candles (*Cimicifuga racemosa*) nod to Alonzo Houser's lady in bronze, framed by the stone wall of Colles and John Larkin's Dellwood, Minnesota, garden. When the wall was built in the 1920s, the opening accommodated an oak tree's large branch.

right ✿ *Conversation Piece, 2001,* by Madrid artist Juan Muñoz, features five bronze figures engaged in "conversation," suggesting both a physical and a verbal tug-of-war. Mounds of boxwood in this Houston garden echo the rounded forms of the figures.

THIS WALL WAS BUILT
1985 – 1987
IN
MEMORY OF
FRANCES TYSON & JOHN BAKER CARSON
WHO LIVED AT TYCA FARM
1930   UNTIL   1979

opposite ✣ British sculptor Barry Flanagan began producing "hare works" in the early 1980s. In *Mirror Nijinsky*, pictured here, he represents the dancer Vaslav Nijinsky and his mirror image, passing a ball back and forth. Visitors to Jean Hudson's Grosse Pointe Farms, Michigan, terrace enjoy the performance.

above ✣ A hound by artist Clayton Bright pursues a fox (page 42) on an ivy-covered wall in the Carsons' garden in Newtown Square, Pennsylvania.

above My love of gardening has led me down more primrose
paths than I care to acknowledge!

Pat Hartrampf, Winfield Farm, Highlands, North Carolina

left ✦ Three cheetahs by South African artist
Shayne Haysom are silhouetted against the
Colorado Springs skyline in Joan Donner's garden.
This group and other sculptures, African in origin,
speak playfully and elegantly of Joan's commitment
to conservation there and her involvement with the
Leakey Foundation.

above ✦ Gathered in the corner of a split-rail fence
on Winfield Farm in Highlands, North Carolina
are *Br'er Fox*, *Br'er Rabbit*, and *Tar-Baby*. The figures, by
a chainsaw carver, were modeled after the original
1880 illustrations by A. B. Frost for Joel Chandler
Harris's *The Uncle Remus Stories*. They remind Pat and
Carl Hartrampf's grandchildren of the many times
their great-grandfather read the stories to them in
the original Southern dialect.

above ✼ Characters from *The Wind in the Willows* live under a tree in Mary and Steven Read's garden in Napa, California. Sculptor Al Guibara created this magical scene from Steven's favorite childhood book, with Ratty and Mole "simply messing around in boats" while Mr. Toad hangs from a nearby bridge. In the spring rainy season, the stream rises to a level that floats the boat.

opposite ✼ This totem pole in Susan Stevenson's Portland, Oregon, garden was commissioned in memory of her late husband, Bruce Stevenson, and carved by artist Mike Olson. It is titled *He Who Wears Many Hats*, a reference to Bruce's diverse talents and energies.

above *My favorite spot is the bench in my small "contemplative" garden. Sitting there even a few minutes has a restorative effect. The longer I am able to stay, the more refined the powers of observation. The more I observe, the greater my appreciation of nature's magical and multilayered world.*

MIMI MCBRIDE, CHEVY CHASE, MARYLAND

opposite ❖ A simple, polished orb echoes the color and smooth texture of a crape myrtle tree (*Lagerstroemia indica*) in Mimi McBride's Chevy Chase, Maryland, garden.

above ❖ A 1983 soapstone sculpture by Hanna Jubran adds its smooth, hard texture to the rough tree bark, the glossy leaves in the hedge, and the sparkling water of the Milwaukee River in Anne and Fred Vogel's Milwaukee, Wisconsin, garden. The artist says he likes his works to be "pleasing to the touch."

above ✿ Jean and Gil Hudson have focused on creating a garden in Grosse Pointe, Michigan, with a "natural and uncomplicated feeling" that would serve as a backdrop for sculptures by Michigan artist Joseph Wesner. The artist said this piece, *Gaulo*, was inspired by the classic Roman sculpture *Dying Gaul*, which he felt embodied the essence of life's conflict with death. The Hudsons say that Wesner was pleased with its garden setting.

left ✿ A contemporary home opens onto a garden with sharply angled hardscape and modern sculpture before giving way to an oak climax forest in Lake Forest, Illinois. The trunk of a nearby tree helps the visitor to see the "tree" in Jesus Moroles's granite *Spirit Tree* in Maxine Hunter's garden.

overleaf ✿ "You might call our outdoors a space of green textures and sculpture," Maxine Hunter says of her Lake Forest, Illinois, garden. "We focused on shade plants and grouped the colors to 'light' dark corners." Native goatsbeard (*Aruncus dioicus*) and the bright red *Spartacus* by Frank Riggs brighten this corner. In the far corner, red astilbe echoes the sculpture's color.

It was a joy to share the garden and the art with so many people, young and old. There were five charity fund-raising events over the four days, with thousands of guests who ate, drank, took photos, and enjoyed themselves, interacting with the art. The glass pieces were not roped off. Visitors could walk among ten-foot-tall red glass reeds, climb the steps where the Green Grass was placed. Most of the events were at night, so the lighting gave a dazzling, magical quality to the art and to the garden.

DIANA NEELY, MEDINA, WASHINGTON

Diana Neely says, "When you say 'yes,' amazing things happen." She said yes to having her Medina, Washington, garden be the site of a marathon of charity functions and to having the renowned Seattle-based glass artist Dale Chihuly exhibit his works of art—on steps, in parterres and trees, even in a boat on the lake. Thirty people from the Chihuly Studio worked for four days installing the glass pieces. Then, for another four days, the garden was filled with one gala charity event after another.

And then it was gone. But Chihuly Studios presented her with a beautiful book of pictures from the exhibition, some shown here, and she has the memories every time she walks in her garden.

opposite ✿ Diana Neely's formal parterre in green and white with a fountain in the middle was the site of choice for Dale Chihuly's *Palazzo Ducale Tower,* 2006—a symmetrical "fountain" of white glass. Photo © Teresa Nouri Rishel.

above left ✿ Chihuly's *Green Grass,* 2006, grows on steps in Diana Neely's garden. Photo © Teresa Nouri Rishel.

above right ✿ Chihuly's *Niijima Float,* 2006, is placed next to the large leaves of ligularia. The white of a nearby azalea is reflected in the float. Photo © Teresa Nouri Rishel.

12 On the Practical Side

WE HAVE SEEN THE MOST GLAMOROUS ASPECTS OF THE GARDEN—THE WELCOMING entrances, glorious views, breathtakingly beautiful borders and beds, color applied with brushes both subtle and bold, microcosms in containers, and those special pleasures of the garden—some large, some very small. In this final chapter we look at the practical side of the garden. However glamorous and meticulously maintained a garden may be, there are some functional matters that need to be addressed.

Where do visitors park?

What do I do with all my tender plants when winter arrives?

Where do we hide the lawn mower and garden cart, the equipment that keeps the swimming pool running?

My grandchildren would love a playhouse. How do I work that into the landscaping plan?

We'd like some chickens. Can you camouflage a chicken coop?

And last, but certainly not least, what about the vegetable garden?

In this chapter, you will see how form has followed function, how garden owners have answered all of these questions with ingenuity while maintaining their garden's appeal.

Perhaps the most interesting solutions will be seen in terms of how vegetable gardens are not just tolerated or even integrated, but instead are featured in the landscape. Susan J. Pennington, in *Feast Your Eyes: The Unexpected Beauty of Vegetable Gardens*, chronicles the rise and fall and rise again of vegetable gardens as an integral part of garden design, an element to be showcased, not hidden. She begins: "Perhaps I should have entitled this book *Ornamental Vegetables: A Budding Cinderella Story.* Ignoring for the moment that it sounds like a headline crafted by a bad sportswriter, I have come to think of the vegetable garden as the Cinderella of the horticultural world—kept around only for the work that she does, her finer attributes outshone by her flashier floral stepsisters."

In America, the earliest settlers were concerned with survival, and they planted seeds they carried with them in walled or fenced enclosures near or attached to the house, which offered protection from predators. What did these garden look like? Denise Otis in *Grounds for Pleasure: Four Centuries of the American Garden* (2002) writes: "We might presume a design of rectangular beds, usually raised, with walks between them as a matter of what one might call folk memory. The earliest illustrations of medieval gardens show just such an organization, which is not so very different from the ancient Persian ones quartered by streams of water. That the Spanish in Florida, the French in Canada, the Dutch in New York, and the English in New England and Virginia all laid out their plant beds to this design is indicated on every map of the period that shows gardens. The same layout went west with the pioneers, and still appeals to many present-day gardeners. It is part of our heritage that we never let go out of fashion very long."

On the following pages, garden owners offer solutions to parking, playhouses, pool houses, wintering over plants—all the practical questions raised earlier. And vegetable gardens take center stage.

previous page ❁ Nasturtiums, trained on trellis towers, await autos and drivers returning to this garage on Mount Desert Island, Maine.

above ❁ The strong sculptural forms of agave and other xeric plants fill a space in tiers of the retaining wall above Carol Valentine's entrance courtyard in Santa Barbara, California.

right ❁ The cottage garden at Read's Leap spills over into the parking area, welcoming visitors and letting them know they are in for a floriferous treat in Mary and Steven Read's Napa, California, garden.

opposite ✣ Ten years ago, when Cecile and Philip McCaull were hosting a family reunion at their home in Greenwich, Connecticut, they installed this playhouse for their granddaughters and a fort for their grandsons. The playhouse was a hit, with both boys and girls. The fort did not get much attention.

above ✣ Anne Coke saw a picture of a Victorian "gingerbready" playhouse in an English gardening magazine and asked her friend, Dallas landscape designer Carl Neels, to copy it. Together they added a room—to the series of rooms in Anne's garden—as a setting. Mondo grass lines the path, and child-size furniture sits near the flower border.

opposite ❖ Herbs and boxwood grow right up to the door of this shed that houses rakes and hoes, hoses and pots, in Carolyn Kroh's garden in Shawnee Mission, Kansas.

top ❖ Two towers of mandevilla vines in Versailles pots mark the door of this structure that houses the pool equipment in Colleen Hempleman's garden in Greenwich, Connecticut.

bottom ❖ Silver fleece vine (*Polygonum aubertii*), climbing 'Peace' rose, and a vigorous stand of red-orange daylilies (*Hemerocallis*) almost hide the potting shed in Holly Brigham's St. Louis, Missouri, garden.

 We now have a dozen chickens. We love the eggs and the great compost. I've gone organic—no more pesticides. I compost chicken manure, leftovers (mostly veggies, fruits, coffee grounds), and garden cuttings. I hope to have "compost tea" soon.

SUE McKINLEY, MONTECITO, CALIFORNIA

When my husband and I were married shortly after World War II, we decided to move out to the family picnic cabin until our rental apartment was available. That was sixty years ago. We never moved to the apartment but have stayed all these years with a home and gardens that have grown like Topsy.

We are still in the country (sixty acres) even though the city now surrounds us. We have a great wealth of flora and fauna— birds, trees, wild animals. We are happy to have bobcats, coyotes, and red fox to help keep the rabbit population down. We have a wonderful abundance of songbirds and a rookery of blue herons with six nests in one huge sycamore. We also have several families of red-tailed hawks, mallard ducks, wood ducks, and a single pair of Canada geese, which I pray will not become a mob.

To prevent complete devastation from the "vegetation eaters," we have found that a single 12-volt wire, at nose height, has been fairly effective in deterring deer. This has worked much better than the ten- to twelve-foot-high fence, without electricity, that we tried earlier. Around the vegetable garden we have added two lower wires to fend off the rabbits, raccoons, and groundhogs.

NORMA SUTHERLAND, SHAWNEE MISSION, KANSAS

left ✿ A friend brought the noted British garden designer Rosemary Verey to lunch at Anne Coke's home in Dallas. When Anne bemoaned the loss of a large tree in her garden, Verey suggested she use the space for a *potager* and proceeded to sketch out a plan. The result is this garden room of formal beds edged with boxwood. Leeks grow in the foreground and the gray foliage of artichokes mixes with delphiniums toward the back. Trellis pyramids and a statue of one of the Seasons add to the formality of the design.

above ✿ The artichokes in grocery stores are the buds of a perennial thistle, *Cynara scolymus,* first cultivated in the Mediterranean area. Here, in Sue McKinley's vegetable garden in Montecito, California, artichokes are beyond the tight bud stage but not yet showing the thistle flower.

right ✿ Most people pick vegetables and take them to the house. Gay Barclay has done just the opposite in Potomac, Maryland. She has taken the house to the vegetables. The stone-and-slat structure in this picture is actually a summer kitchen, complete with stove, sink, refrigerator, and icemaker. Vegetables go from her raised beds to stir-fry to table in a matter of minutes. A dining "room" and living "room" are nearby. (See page 72.)

overleaf, left ✿ The beds in Gwen Babcock's San Marino, California, garden are raised and the paths are concrete to enable her to plant, weed, and harvest from her electric wheelchair.

overleaf, right ✿ Pretty as a picture is the Wister garden in Hunterdon County, New Jersey. An elegant white fence frames blocks of color— chartreuse to blue-green—and textures from fuzzy to metallic shiny. A sundial on a pedestal marks the center axis.

I have been a gardener since childhood. Having had polio at the age of seven, I was unable to ride a bike or play sports, so I would work in my section of my family's garden when I was home from school. In those days I got around on crutches and could walk around my garden. For the past fifteen years I have been in an electric wheelchair and have found it easier for me to enjoy all gardens this way. I can also move pots a lot easier.

GWEN BABCOCK, SAN MARINO, CALIFORNIA

248

left ✿ Hard to believe that weeds hid these rows of large boxwoods when the Whitmores bought Langdon Farm in 1993. Now the box does what it was intended to do when planted in the 1920s— edge a garden room, in this case the vegetable and cutting garden. Langdon Farm is in the tiny hamlet of Sherwood, Maryland. Espaliered fruit trees, planted for the couple's thirtieth wedding anniversary, march down the left side in front of cold frames. Beyond the box hedge, the property lives up to its farm name, with a field of soy reaching out to Harris Creek on Chesapeake Bay. Other crops on the 150 acres are corn and winter wheat. An American *ferme ornée,* surely.

251

Bibliography

Abell, Sam, *Seeing Gardens*. Washington, D. C.: National Geographic Society, 2000.

Archer-Wills, Anthony, *Designing Water Gardens: A Unique Approach*. London: Conran Octopus, 1999.

Beckett, Kenneth, David Carr, and David Stevens, *The Contained Garden: A Complete Illustrated Guide to Growing Plants, Flowers, Fruits, and Vegetables Outdoors in Pots*. (First published by Frances Lincoln Limited, London, 1982.) New York: Viking Penguin, 1993.

Brickell, Christopher, and Judith D. Zuk, eds., *The American Horticultural Society A–Z Encyclopedia of Garden Plants*. New York: Dorling Kindersley, 1996.

Cabot, Francis H., *The Greater Perfection: The Story of the Gardens at Les Quatre Vents*. New York: W.W. Norton, 2001.

Church, Thomas D., Grace Hall, and Michael Laurie, *Gardens Are for People*, second edition. (Originally published by Reinhold Publishing Corporation, New York, 1955.) New York: McGraw-Hill, 1983.

Cox, Jeff, and Marilyn Cox, *The Perennial Garden: Color Harmonies Through the Seasons*. Emmaus, Pennsylvania: Rodale, 1985.

Crowe, Sylvia, *Garden Design*. New York: Hearthside, 1959.

Dickey, Page, *Breaking Ground: Garden Design Solutions from Ten Contemporary Masters*. New York: Artisan, 1997.

Don, Montagu, *The Sensuous Garden*. New York: Simon and Schuster, 1997.

Drower, George, *Garden of Invention*. (Originally published by Sutton Publishing, Stroud, England, as *Gardeners, Gurus, and Grubs*, 2001.) Guilford, Connecticut: First Lyons, revised edition, 2003.

Druse, Ken, *The Collector's Garden: Designing with Extraordinary Plants*. New York: Clarkson Potter, 1996.

Ellis, Barbara W., *Taylor's Guide to Perennials*. New York: Houghton Mifflin, 2000.

Forster, Roy, and Alex Downie, *The Woodland Garden: Planting in Harmony with Nature*, revised edition. (Originally published by Raincoast, Vancouver, British Columbia.) Buffalo, New York: Firefly, 2004.

Grimshaw, Dr. John, *The Gardener's Atlas: The Origins, Discovery, and Cultivation of the World's Most Popular Garden Plants*. Willowdale, Ontario: Firefly, 1998.

Griswold, Mac, and Eleanor Weller, *The Golden Age of American Gardens: Proud Owners, Private Estates, 1890–1940*. New York: Harry N. Abrams, 1991.

Hobhouse, Penelope, *The Story of Gardening*. London: Dorling Kindersley, 2001.

—— *In Search of Paradise: Great Gardens of the World*. London: Frances Lincoln, 2006.

—— and Elvin McDonald, eds., *Gardens of the World: The Art and Practice of Gardening*. New York: Macmillan, 1991.

Jekyll, Gertrude, *Colour Schemes for the Flower Garden: Introduced and Revised by Graham Stuart Thomas*. (Originally published by Country Life, London.) Salem, New Hampshire: Ayer, 1983.

—— *On Gardening*. Edited with a commentary by Penelope Hobhouse. Boston: David R. Godine, Publisher, 1983.

Jellicoe, Sir Geoffrey, Susan Jellicoe, Patrick Goode, and Michael Lancaster, eds., *The Oxford Companion to Gardens*. Oxford: Oxford University Press, 1991.

Johnson, Hugh, *Principles of Gardening: The Practice of the Gardener's Art*. New York: Simon and Schuster, 1993.

Lamb, Christian, *From the Ends of the Earth*. Devon, England: Bene Factum, 2004.

Le Toquin, Alain, *The Most Beautiful Gardens in the World*. New York: Harry N. Abrams, 2004.

Leighton, Ann, *Early American Gardens: "For Meate or Medicine."* New York: Cassell, 1970.

—— *American Gardens in the Eighteenth Century: "For Use or for Delight."* (Originally published Houghton Mifflin, Boston, 1976.) Amherst: University of Massachusetts Press, 1988.

Lockwood, Alice G. B., *Gardens of Colony and State: Gardens and Gardeners of the American Colonies and of the Republic Before 1840*, two vols.; new edition. (Originally published in the 1930s.) New York: Smallwood and Stewart for The Garden Club of America, 2000.

Lovejoy, Ann, *American Mixed Border: A Garden for All Seasons*. New York: Macmillan, 1993.

Loudon, J. C., *An Encyclopaedia of Gardening; Comprising the Theory and Practice of Horticulture, Floriculture, Arboriculture, and Landscape Gardening . . .*; new edition edited by Mrs. Loudon. London: Longman, Green, Longman, and Roberts, 1860.

Mackinnon, Nancy Ballek, *The Gardener's Book of Charts, Tables & Lists*. Sterling, Virginia: Capital, 2002.

Nollman, Jim, *Why We Garden: Cultivating a Sense of Place*. (First published by Henry Holt, New York.) Boulder, Colorado: First Sentient, 2005.

Ockenga, Starr, *Earth on Her Hands: The American Woman in Her Garden*. New York: Clarkson Potter, 1998.

—— *Eden on Their Minds: American Gardeners with Bold Visions*. New York: Clarkson Potter, 2001.

Otis, Denise, *Grounds for Pleasure: Four Centuries of the American Garden*. New York: Harry N. Abrams, 2002.

Page, Russell, *The Education of a Gardener*. (First published by William Collins and Sons, Glasgow, 1962.) New York: New York Review Books, 1994.

Pennington, Susan J., *Feast Your Eyes: The Unexpected Beauty of Vegetable Gardens*. Berkeley and Los Angeles: University of California Press, 2004.

Pollan, Michael, *Second Nature: A Gardener's Education*. New York: Grove, 1991.

Power, Nancy Goslee, *The Gardens of California: Four Centuries of Design from Mission to Modern*. New York: Clarkson Potter, 1995.

Schinz, Marina, and Susan Littlefield, *Visions of Paradise: Themes and Variations in the Garden*. New York: Stewart, Tabori & Chang, 1985.

Shulman, Nicola, *A Rage for Rock Gardening: The Story of Reginald Farrer: Gardener, Writer & Plant Collector*. Boston: David R. Godine, 2004.

Taylor, Patrick, ed., *The Oxford Companion to the Garden*. Oxford: Oxford University Press, 2006.

Thaxter, Celia, *An Island Garden*. (Originally published 1894 by Houghton Mifflin.) Boston: Houghton Mifflin, 1988.

Tilden, Scott J., ed., *The Glory of Gardens: 2000 Years of Writings on Garden Design*. New York: Harry N. Abrams, 2006.

Verey, Rosemary, *Rosemary Verey's Making of a Garden*. London: Frances Lincoln, 1995.

Whittle, Tyler, *The Plant Hunters . . . .* New York: PAJ, 1988.

Wilson, Andrew, *Influential Gardeners: Designers Who Shaped Twentieth-Century Garden Style*. New York: Clarkson Potter, 2002.

Winterrowd, Wayne, ed., *Roses: A Celebration*. New York: North Point, 2003.

Woods, May, and Arethe Swartz Warren, *Glass Houses: A History of Greenhouses, Orangeries and Conservatories*. London: Aurum, 1988.

Index

Acknowledgments

OUR FIRST "THANK YOU NOTE" MUST GO TO MARGARET L. KAPLAN, EDITOR-AT-LARGE at Harry N. Abrams, Inc., who worked with Bonny Martin and me on *The Fine Art of Flower Arranging*. Early in the planning stages of that book, Margaret envisioned a sequel featuring members' gardens, and has continued to inspire and guide us at every stage along the way. Our second note surely goes to photographer Mick Hales, who forgave and forgot the stresses of the first book and said it would be an honor to work on this one. And our third goes to those ninety-plus members who returned Bonny's phone calls and said they would be happy to have Mick photograph their gardens for a Garden Club of America book.

Darilyn Carnes, designer extraordinaire, took these efforts and talents and turned them into a work of art that has exceeded our highest expectations. Thank you, Darilyn. You have made the concept of a "visiting garden tour" a virtual reality.

Through it all, Nancy Murray has been our liaison to the Executive Committee, communicating our goals and eliciting their unwavering and much appreciated support. Thank you, Nancy and Exec.

Beyond this most obvious phalanx are dozens of people who helped in so many ways, especially in identifying the gardens to be photographed. In Bonny's words: "I am deeply indebted to the members who helped me find these gardens. If I name names, I will inadvertently leave out many. You know who you are, and we are deeply grateful. My husband, David, too, must be thanked for his support, even when the phone rang during dinner. I would answer, hoping it was a returned call from someone I had been trying to reach for days, and often it was. Thank you, garden owners, and to all who helped me identify these outstanding gardens."

My own husband, Woody, planned every facet of the trips we made to meet Mick in twenty gardens. It was an assignment I could not have done without him.

Along the route, I am particularly grateful to members who extended their thoughtful assistance and hospitality to us and to Mick Hales—Lillian Balentine Law in Atlanta and Lake Toxaway, North Carolina; and in California, Fran Neumann in San Marino, Pamela Smith in Carmel-by-the-Sea, and Phoebe Gilpin in Hillsborough. I am grateful to Tricia Albus and the GCA Library Committee for making the very rare *Encyclopaedia of Gardening* by J. C. Loudon available to me, and to the staff of the Portland Library for tracking down all manner of garden books. I also thank Nancy Ballek Mackinnon, Elaine Carella, and Joanne Lendon for their willing assistance.

My family was enthusiastic and wonderfully supportive. Son-in-law Thomas Jenei programmed a new MacBook to respond to my every wish. Daughter Sarah, an equine veterinarian, found "the most beautiful garden" while making a barn call in Massachusetts. And San Francisco daughter Susannah supplied almost daily encouragement and technical assistance by phone, and lent her good company and lunch-acquiring skills to several sites in California.

A final thank you must go to the Middletown Garden Club, whose members have, for thirty-five years, raised my awareness of things beautiful and important on this fragile planet.

Nancy D'Oench
March 2008

Editor: Margaret L. Kaplan
Designer: Darilyn Lowe Carnes
Production Manager: Jules Thomson

Library of Congress Cataloging-in-Publication Data:

D'Oench, Nancy.
  Gardens private and personal : a Garden Club of America book / text by Nancy
D'Oench; coordination by Bonny Martin; photography by Mick Hales.
    p. cm.
  ISBN 978-0-8109-7280-3
  1. Gardens—United States. 2. Gardens—United States—Pictorial works. 3.
Gardens—United States—Design. 4. Gardens—United
States—Design—Pictorial works. I. Martin, Bonny. II. Hales, Mick. III.
Garden Club of America. IV. Title.

  SB466.U6D64 2008
  712.0973—dc22

            2007049003

Published in 2008 by Abrams, an imprint of Harry N. Abrams, Inc.

For information about special discounts for bulk purchases, please contact
Harry N. Abrams Special Sales at specialsales@hnabooks.com or phone 212-229-7109.

Printed and bound in China
10 9 8 7 6 5 4 3 2 1

harry n. abrams, inc.
a subsidiary of La Martinière Groupe
115 West 18th Street
New York, NY 10011
www.hnabooks.com

page 1 ✿ Twenty-five years ago, Bettie Beardon
Pardee saw a bench with interlocking initials at Birr
Castle in County Offaly, Ireland. She had this one
made for her Newport garden, and it quickly won
her cat's approval. Photo © Bettie Beardon Pardee.

page 2-3 ✿ Sometimes the best view is an aerial
one, as it is here, looking down on a knot garden
that features a variety of sages centered around a
topiary of rosemary outside a pool house in Illinois.

page 4 ✿ Standing amid several varieties of native
yucca and a fruiting loquat in Judy Tate's Houston
garden is a rhinoceros of Italian limestone. The
figure, made by artisans in Vicenza, Italy, interprets
an Albrecht Dürer drawing from the sixteenth
century.